KERB 27

Journal of Landscape Architecture

2019

••

Kerb is published annually by Uro Publications, Melbourne, Victoria
uropublications.com.

ISBN 978-0-6484355-7-0
ISSN 1324-8049

Printed in Singapore.

Distributed in Australia by Books at Manic and internationally by Idea Books.

Each edition of Kerb is produced by a new student editorial team.

••

Editors
Benjamin Jameson
Emily Sinyavker
Gary Ward
Reuben Chan
Shanley Price

Managing editor
Charles Anderson

Supervising editor
Ricky Ray Ricardo

Production consultants
Karina Smith - Kerb 27 Copy Editor
Sally Holdsworth - Kerb 27 Copy Editor

••

Art direction
Sean Hogan - Trampoline

Graphic design
A collaboration between the editors and Sean Hogan - Trampoline
trampoline.net.au

Acknowledgments
The editors would like to thank everyone involved in the production of the journal for their generous assistance and support during the process of this publication.

••

Sponsors

Silver

Taylor. Cullity. Lethlean

OCULUS

Bronze

Hansen Partnership

Friend

Sue Barnsley Design

Front cover illustration:
Jieun Lee
leegoc.com
instagram: leegoc

S E L E C T I V E

Who are we really designing for?

P E R C E P T I O N S

Contents

Editorial

Benjamin Jameson
Emily Sinyavker
Gary Ward
Reuben Chan
Shanley Price

The spaces we inhabit in our daily lives have been designed for people, but have they been designed for you?

There is a swathe of agendas embedded in the design process. They are predicated on who is setting out the brief, where it is in space, the political climate at the time, and the desired uses. Often in these designs particular people are designed for, and others are designed out. Throughout the design process designers can be complicit in, oblivious to, or supportive of the political agendas of the client.

This issue of *Kerb* poses two critical questions: firstly, whose responsibility is it to make sure that public spaces are accessible to all, especially those who are marginalised? And secondly, what influence can and do designers have over these outcomes? This complexity and tension is realised in the diversity of submissions, and is key in particular contributions.

Who is included in a space, and how, is largely dependent on the tools the designer has in their toolkit. Beyond our drawing conventions, software, and pen case, there are tools we can use that are less tangible. In our interview with him, Walter Hood called for landscape architects to increase their social theory literacy. It is this literacy, he argues, that is the key to us making unique, sensitive and valued landscapes, but that we are severely lacking as a discipline. Danielle Toronyi's submission walks a similar line. Her work helps to communicate the experiences of people with neurodivergent conditions in a city to designers of urban space. Toronyi's visual representation of sensorial perceptions gives neurotypical people a sense of the experiences of someone with autism. Without these tools, designers are unable to generate sensitive and valued landscapes, or work against the often hegemonic campaigns by private developers.

The Forest City project in Malaysia is reclaiming tracts of seagrass beds to "develop" the land into housing for 700,000 residents. Among other things, the project's master plan intends to protect the seagrass ecosystem that local fishermen rely on. Just who the residents will be is unclear, as the local Malaysian fishermen cannot afford to live in the development.

What is interesting here is the hierarchy of considerations in this project. Forest City sits within a wider context of neo-imperial, capitalist agendas, and the dichotomy between corporate master plans and the lived experience of people.

This dichotomy reveals itself time and time again. There are pertinent questions to ask, especially when considering who is involved and, more importantly, what is lost when marginalised voices are shut out of the conversation.

Brent Greene and Abigail Varney show us how inviting queer readings of a space can open the conceived range of a landscape, and can work to remedy even the arguably failed capitalist landscape of the Docklands, Melbourne. Further, a piece by Lois Nguyen argues that disabled experiences are being designed out of urban space by the focus on legally mandated disability access requirements. Further, she argues that in doing so we are missing out on a challenging and exciting design question – how to design for diversity in physical experience (beyond a designated slope gradient or handrails). Both works highlight to us the value of involving traditionally marginalised voices in our design process, not only to ensure inclusiveness, but also for the wider benefits this brings to our designs.

Greene and Varney present a version of queerness in space that while subversive, doesn't portray acts of queerness in space to be dangerous acts. In contrast, Eloise Choquette presents a story where being queer in a public space was a life or liberty endangering act.

Ironically, it has not always been so easy to be radically different in public (space). Choquette's work highlights the struggles of the people who sit on the fringes of society almost a century ago with the Caravan Club, a safe space for queer identifing people that was consistently on the verge of closure and under surveillance. Yet today we continue to speak about the need for safe spaces for the queer community and other marginalised groups. In their struggle, we can learn about the courage to take action. It is because of them that we can enjoy the (limited) freedom we have today, and can push the goalposts even further.

As designers, if we are pushing for change, it is not enough to only passively read and talk, we must be bold, make claims and take action. This issue of *Kerb* provides us with an opportunity to better learn about the people around us, and to consider new ways to think about our designs. Further, this edition contributes to a wider call for action. In the words of Choquette's submission, 'We must understand [design] from a different stance, as part of a wider, even more complex system. We cannot hope to change the way we design if we do not also work, continuously, to dismantle capitalism, racism and the patriarchy'.

ABSTRACT

The exclusivity of urban assemblage has granted access to only a select few, and only in select ways.

Cities house some of the most diverse populations, while paradoxically, corporate buy-in has created an increasingly homogenous built environment. Design that does not consider the diversity of its community produces a narrow outcome, and decision makers are at risk of becoming increasingly abstracted from their constituents.

In effect, this deepens the exclusion of particular populations from our cities, and reproduces predetermined outcomes, based on narrow and biased perspectives. We all have the capacity and responsibility to contribute to, and be aware of, the world we are designing. Structural inequity promotes race- class- gender- age- ability- sexuality-based exclusion, whose effects multiply throughout society. How should and do designers address this context through their practise?

Design should be for the people, both the expected and the unexpected user. We should be empathetic, open and accountable. Does that really reflect how work is done or valued today? How are design professions responding to this tension, and what are the consequences if they don't?

Contemporary society is approaching a reckoning of identity, to which designers will have to respond. *Kerb* 27 addresses issues of inequity in our built and social environments, and asks the question: Who are we really designing for?

Danielle **Toronyi**

NEURODIVERSITY IN THE SENSORIAL CITY

'Autistic people face exclusion from public life due to the design of the urban realm and public space of which the sensory and auditory qualities are not considered.'

Autistic people are often hypersensitive to sensory constructions of space. When confronted with unexpected, new or multisensory information this hypersensitivity often causes extreme distress. Autistic people face exclusion from public life due to the design of the urban realm and public space of which the sensory and auditory qualities are not considered. Can cities be sensorially and acoustically accessible to autistic or otherwise neurodivergent people?

Here, a research methodology is presented which provides a critical opportunity for landscape architects and urban designers to work with, learn from and design for autistic people by removing acoustic and sensorial barriers to the urban environment. The proposed methodology is comprised of ethnographic field recordings and embodied kinesthetic evaluations of urban space, collected through sensory walks and interviews, as well as sound mapping studies and field recordings. This process is informed by Lawrence and Anna Halprin's work in the RSVP cycles and Taking Part collaborative workshops, which stressed citizen participation and which serve as a model for an exploratory, sensorial analysis of the urban environment. The resultant ethnographic materials constitute a new inventory of the city by representing autistic and neurodivergent ways of sensing, hearing and knowing the urban environment.

Introduction

Landscape architects and urban designers are tasked with the critical responsibility to design inclusive and accessible environments for all users, including those with physical, sensory, developmental or cognitive disabilities. Since 1990 in the United States, the *Americans with Disabilities Act* has required that the built environment meet the needs of the majority of those with physical disabilities and/or people who use mobility devices. More recently, 'universal design' has expanded the understanding of accessibility and inclusivity. The autistic and neurodivergent community is one of many underserved disabled communities whose needs are not addressed in ADA standards or in universal design.

Autism and neurodivergence

The term neurodivergent describes someone whose neurocognitive functioning does not align with existing social norms. Autism Spectrum Disorder (ASD) is a developmental disorder and, within the neurodivergent and 'actually autistic' communities, is considered one of many neurological variations. Occurring in both children and adults throughout the world, it may be more common than originally thought. While the medical community does not know why the occurrence rates of autism in both children and adults are increasing, many researchers confirm that greater awareness, improved case identification and changes in the age of diagnosis, as well as changing diagnostic factors have a significant impact on the occurrence rate.[1]

Hypersensitivity to sound is one of the most common sensory processing dysfunctions experienced by autistic people.[2] In addition to difficulties with social interaction, communication challenges, and engaging in repetitive behaviours, sensory processing disorder

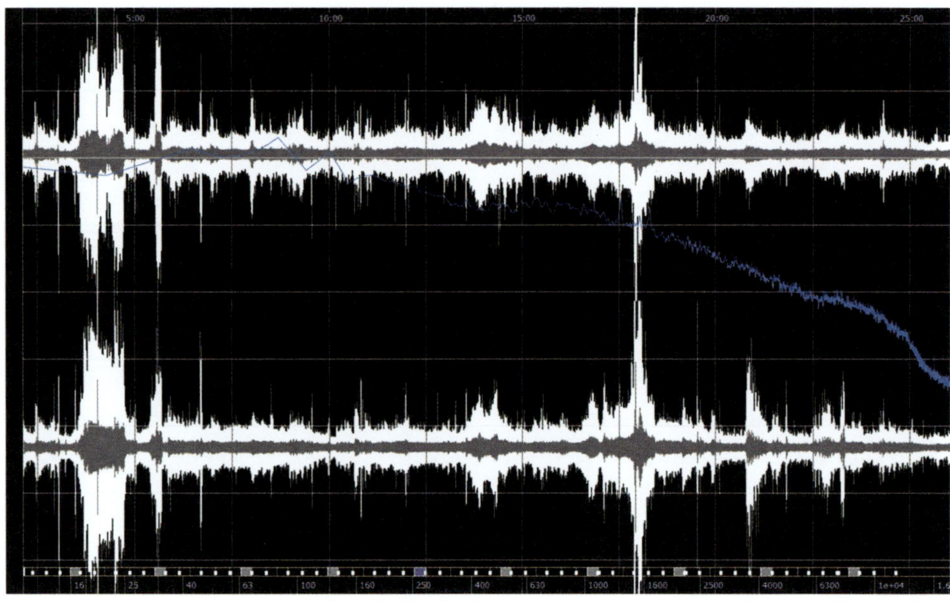

Fig. 1 Visual assessment of field recording with Sonic Visualizer software conducted in May 2019 in Center City, Philadelphia. WAV file with spectrum visualisation (showing frequencies along the x axis).

is a common symptom of ASD. Recent studies have revealed that autistic people, both adults and children, may share a similar dysfunction in the part of the brain that regulates perception and the integration of complex sounds.[3] Within the sensory world of cities, sound may be the most pervasive and impactful sensation for autistic people.

Currently, there is no standard set of design guidelines that addresses the design of the public commons or urban space to accommodate the needs of autistic people. In 2015, Magda Mostafa created the Autism ASPECTSS™ Design Index[4] which establishes a design framework for architects that seeks to create a standardised treatment of interior space. While the Autism ASPECTSS™ Design Index organises an evidence-based framework for interior spaces, these practices have not been applied in the landscape. The current state of neurodivergent landscape architecture research is focused on private outdoor places for children, such as small-scale horticulture therapy gardens in private healthcare settings, niche residential design and private educational play spaces. While architects and landscape architects have started to understand how autistic children experience and respond to the constructed environment, urban design has not been analysed in order to design places that are sensorially and acoustically accessible to autistic or otherwise neurodivergent people.

Research proposal – Hidden Geographies

Hidden Geographies is a research project proposal that invites autistic or otherwise neurodivergent people to explore the visual, spatial and acoustic qualities of public space via a community-based participatory research process. Autistic people are particularly well-suited to participate in such a research project, and evidence suggests that their inclusion is required for more accurate representation.

In *Hidden Geographies*, autistic people will explore, via an embodied and sensorial ethnography, the visual, spatial and sonic qualities of public space. *Hidden Geographies* invites neurotypical designers to enter into the autistic way of knowing, perceiving and embodying place - entering into the hidden geographies of sensation. Designing this ethnographic study to include the body of the researcher and researched as part of the process of inquiry and data collection affords a 'greater phenomenological sensibility to ethnography'.[5] These hidden geographies provide critical information for developing new ways to envision urban design. The resultant ethnographic materials constitute a new inventory of the city - representing autistic and neurodivergent ways of knowing and being in the urban environment.

The methods of this proposed community-based ethnographic study are rooted in interviews, field recordings, and sensory and sound mapping. Field recording allows the participants to directly capture acoustic phenomena; sounds that are pleasant or compelling, intriguing and melodic, or frightening and overwhelming. Individual field recordings provide a direct representation of moving through linear time within a site. Visual analysis of sound files offers a new way of conceptualising the landscape and experience of site (Fig. 1). Spatialising the field recordings and particular points of

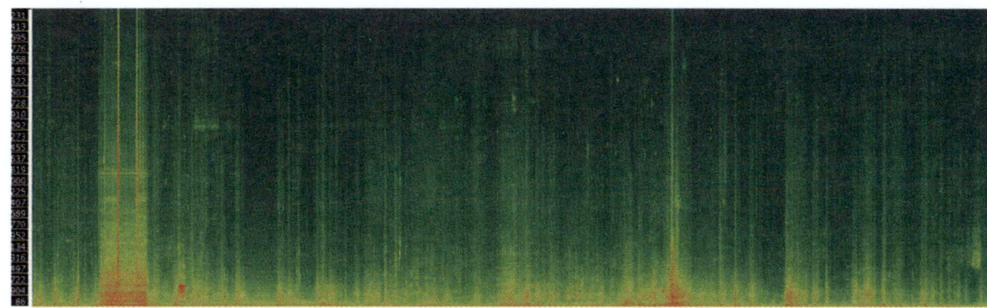

Fig. 2 Spectrogram (visualising the amplitude across a range of frequencies including both background noise and equalisation).

Fig. 3 Melodic range spectrogram (illustrating meaningful acoustic events).

sensation (into a series of sound maps), combined with interviews, will lend designers insight as to where we can more closely explore the composition of urban design elements that have caused a sensory reaction.

This process is inspired by the geographic research field that uses the body as a research tool, in order to more deeply know and engage with place.[6] Human geography teaches us how a walk translates into an embodied engagement: '[t]o walk through a place is to become involved in that place with sight, hearing, touch, smell... proprioception, and even taste'.[7] This process is additionally informed by Lawrence and Anna Halprin's work. Their RSVP cycles and Taking Part collaborative workshops, *Experiments in Environment,* stress citizen participation and provide a useful model for an exploratory, sensorial analysis of the urban environment.[8]

Conclusion

The primary goal of this research project is to recognise and improve the lived experience and clinical outcomes of autistic people; however, as an ethnographic study of autistic people's experience in the city this project provides a significant opportunity to share autistic stories and experiences across a broad field of scholarship. Not only will we serve the physical, sensory and cognitive needs of autistic people, but we will also garner acceptance, accommodation and advocacy for autistic people in the built environment. Additionally, this project has the potential to shift disability discourse within the design professions from the medical model to social model, and work to build a world that is accommodating to all abilities.

By explicitly designing for autism in public space, we invite autistic people to engage more fully in our community and lessen the social oppression facing autistic people, based in stigma and fear. Landscape architects can challenge the prevailing social norms surrounding disability by removing social and physical barriers to full social inclusion. Working to remove barriers to public space, and designing for all experiences, landscape architects can advocate for the recognition of humanity and equality in all of our community members.

LEARNING FROM THE SHIM SHAM CLUB

Eloise Choquette

Architects are not the only ones who transform space. They may lay the first stone, draw the first line, yet they rarely take into account the agency of other people to transform space and architecture. Go to any park, anywhere in the world and there will always be 'desire paths' straying away from the paved paths. People continue to transform the carefully designed structure long after the contractors finish the building work, the inauguration ceremonies, the flashy pictures in magazines.

Architecture is rarely designed for the marginalised. Then and now, the ruling classes build as many monuments to their own self importance as they can. Architecture is complicit – it's always been a tool of oppression, of colonialism, of power. With the fast progression of capitalism in the past century, architecture has become a fast commodity. There seems to be a continuous need to build taller, faster, cheaper structures, in ever greater quantities - and think less and less.

The isolated projects that address inequity are often furthering another hidden agenda to gain political leverage or largely ignored by the media in favour of more flamboyant projects. Profitability and return on investment are what drive projects and the building industry. Projects addressing the dire need for social housing and inequities in accessibility are scarce, and the divide between the affluent and the rest keeps widening. How can shelters, social housing and accessibility compete with the glamour of the dizzyingly tall skyscrapers of Dubai and the extravagant opera houses, libraries and museums? 'Starchitects' design buildings, like Hollywood produces blockbusters, with teams composed of: mostly white, straight, cisgender, able-bodied men – if not exclusively.

It shouldn't be surprising that the most successful examples of mixed, inclusive spaces are not the product of architects, but originated from grassroots organisations and social justice movements. Liminal spaces, in-between spaces, existing on the edge of the visible, of the affluent, of the well-designed, will always thrive and survive, unbeknownst to most – no matter how hard politicians, promoters, city planners and architects try to clean and sanitise cities. As Jeff Goldblum's character, Dr Ian Malcolm, says in *Jurassic Park*, 'Life, uh, finds a way'.

These liminal places are precious; they often are the only safe spaces around for the radical, the marginal, the marginalised. They are precious, and yet precarious. They are always seconds away from being made illegal, from being torn down by promoters and institutions. Their successful survival, though, does not reside in the physical space they occupy. Indeed, these safe spaces move around continuously, clandestinely – they are made possible, exist, because of the people who create them. The notions of space and architecture become moot; potentially, any structure could be used, as long as the people who use it are there, and make it their own, adapt it to their needs.

Occupying these invisible spaces becomes an act of transgression, of resistance in a society that constantly tries to push white supremacy and heteronormativity. It's hard to study precedents as many of these spaces were dismantled in haste or simply not deemed important enough to be documented. Though archives are scarce, a few good examples still made their way through history, such as the Caravan Club and Shim Sham Club, non-heteronormative gathering spaces that operated in 1930s London – a time when being openly gay or trans could result in extreme legal consequences.

A complaint against the Shim Sham Club, from 'a neighbour of Wardour Street', which was investigated by the police, 1935. The National Archives (UK). Catalogue reference: MEPO 2/4494

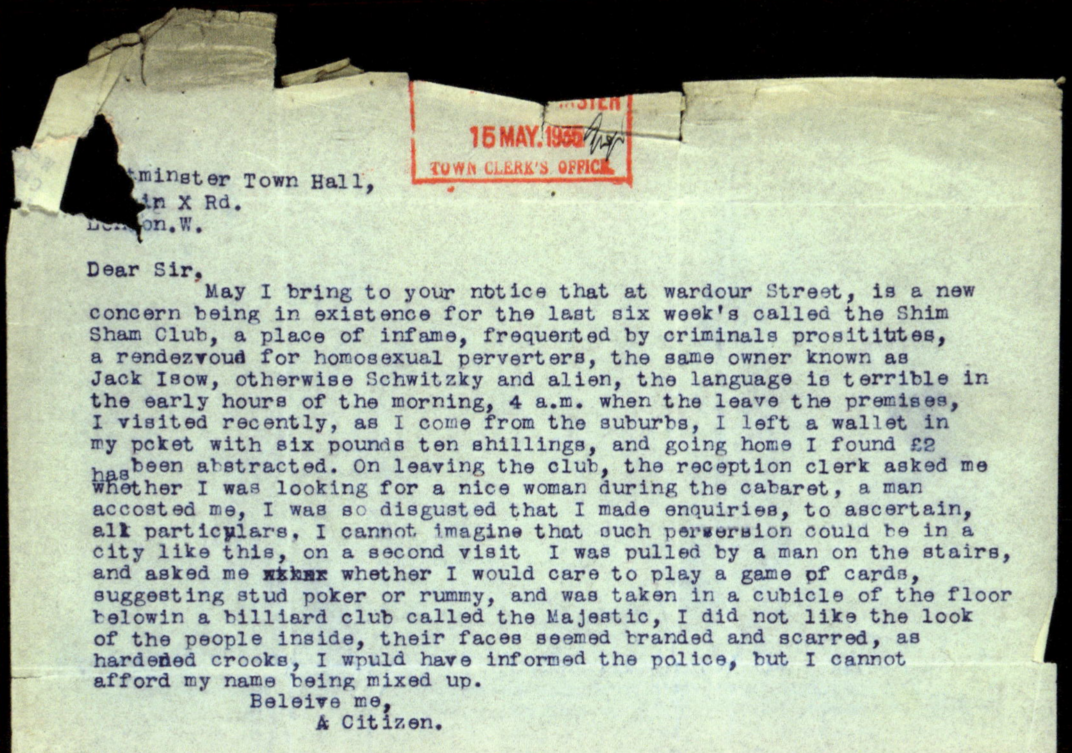

15 MAY.1935
TOWN CLERK'S OFFICE

minster Town Hall,
in X Rd.
on.W.

Dear Sir,
May I bring to your ntice that at wardour Street, is a new concern being in existence for the last six week's called the Shim Sham Club, a place of infame, frequented by criminals prosititutes, a rendezvoud for homosexual perverters, the same owner known as Jack Isow, otherwise Schwitzky and alien, the language is terrible in the early hours of the morning, 4 a.m. when the leave the premises, I visited recently, as I come from the suburbs, I left a wallet in my poket with six pounds ten shillings, and going home I found £2 has been abstracted. On leaving the club, the reception clerk asked me whether I was looking for a nice woman during the cabaret, a man accosted me, I was so disgusted that I made enquiries, to ascertain, all particulars, I cannot imagine that such perversion could be in a city like this, on a second visit I was pulled by a man on the stairs, and asked me whether I would care to play a game of cards, suggesting stud poker or rummy, and was taken in a cubicle of the floor belowin a billiard club called the Majestic, I did not like the look of the people inside, their faces seemed branded and scarred, as hardened crooks, I wpuld have informed the police, but I cannot afford my name being mixed up.

Beleive me,
A Citizen.

The Caravan Club.
The National Archives (UK)

'As architects, we need to stop and listen to the people for whom we are designing, but also to the people who will coexist with the architectures we are building.'

For years, these clubs, like every other club of their kind, were under surveillance by the local authorities. The Caravan was shut down in 1934, after a raid that resulted in the arrest of more than a hundred people.[1] Similarly, soon after its opening in 1935, the Shim Sham Club was reported to police by neighbours for illegal activities that were also deemed immoral. Through it all, the Shim Sham Club succeeded in remaining unregistered until it was shut down.[2]

Nowadays, similar spaces are often 'do-it-yourself' (DIY) spaces organised directly by the people who use them - in a reaction to officially sanctioned spaces and architectures defined by government and social norms. DIY creates safer spaces for people with marginalised identities, such as black, Indigenous, people of colour, queer, trans and gender nonconforming, working class, disabled, and all the intersections of these identities dramatically underrepresented in the construction industry. They become places of radical acceptance - in constant motion and evolution, and in combination with their ephemerality and their illegality they become adaptable, portable, and sustainable in ways that public spaces are usually incapable of.

It's as though these 'non-places' come alive through the progressive nature of the thinking and politics associated with them. Architects and designers would benefit from studying these liminal spaces, as they are ruthlessly honest, self-aware, and critical. They are seemingly chaotic when compared to the familiar, well aligned rows of houses and orthogonal condos familiar to our cities, and yet they serve their function well. They are flexible in a way that most buildings would benefit from.

Learning from these forgotten spaces and people in our society, we should focus on how we build and design rather than on the buildings and designs themselves. After all, as Audre Lorde wrote, 'the master's tools will never dismantle the master's house'. 'They may allow us to temporarily beat him at his own game, but they will never enable us to bring about genuine change'.[3] As architects, we have been given tools and skills that have been passed down for generations; and while these skills and tools can help the people around us we need to start using them more critically. We need to pause more often, to question ourselves, the way things are done, and for whom they are done for. We need to challenge the status quo, the politicians with delusions of grandeur, and the promoters of dollar signs.

We must understand architecture as part of a complex system. We cannot hope to change the way we design if we do not also work, continuously, to dismantle capitalism, racism and the patriarchy. As architects we need to stop and listen not only to the people for whom we are designing, but also to the people who will coexist with the architecture we are building. We need to pause, think, and ask ourselves: just because we could, does it mean that we should?

Marginalised people thriving beyond the city landscapes, above it - not under it. Artwork by Sam Leighton-Dore.

Interview with Walter Hood

Kerb 27 Editorial Team

Kerb attended the Landscape Australia Conference in May, 2019. One of our editors, Ben Jameson, sat down with Walter Hood, creative director and founder of Hood Design Studio, and a professor of landscape architecture at the University of California, Berkeley. They spoke about identity, cultural literacy and design.

Image credit: Hood Design Studio.

'Culture is messy, and politics is hard to talk about, especially when you've never had the vocabulary to do so. If a syllabus never includes Foucault, or gender studies, students are not being equipped to think or talk about complex, important issues. In their place, normative values become prominent, and deny the idea that there can be difference.'

'I was just in South Africa and landscape architects in Cape Town are doing drawings like the kids from Penn, and ... kids from Hong Kong are making drawings like kids from Oakland. And I'm like *where is the cultural discourse?*' Hood remarked, when talking about the simultaneous importance but lack of cultural studies in landscape architecture courses internationally.

In the advancement of the discipline landscape architecture needs to embrace big political ideas and respond to them in a nuanced way. Hood embodies this need – and this truth. Through both his presentation and interview with us, he demonstrates just how landscape architects can broach political topics, and how politics can be and is embedded in (public) space.

BJ: *Why did you start your practice and did you feel a need to be able to do your own, meaningful work?*

WH: My practice came out of academia. I started out teaching and I had to have a way to talk about research; and, as a designer my design, my work, is my research. The studio started out as a practice that was research orientated. So through that I could then articulate a vision for how I wanted to practice, and then have a pedagogy that allowed me to disseminate that information, either through lectures or to my students. And so, very early, the practice started out in this kind of way, to articulate a set of values, a set of ideas.

BJ: *You talked [in the presentation] about the last 'free' open public space in San Francisco. What did you mean by that?*

WH: I was considering that with the high cost of living, people are becoming more transient. The parks are probably going to be the only democratised space left. The bay area is becoming hyper-expensive and our parks, particularly the larger ones that sit in these environments, are going to be the last places where people will feel like they're welcome.

BJ: *Obviously your work touches on significant political topics. I understand you're writing a book. What issue(s) does it cover and what is it about?*

WH: It's called *Hybrid Landscapes* and it takes the position of looking at ecological history and valuing the idea that landscapes are already transforming, meaning that there is no return to origins in a new way.

If we look at landscapes as being in a place that's already formed, they're just going to continue to form and whether we bring ideas that take us backwards, there's still going to be this push to go forward. We see that with sea level rise, we see that with the global change of climates, but still we keep wanting to go backwards. The hybrid allows us to be articulate about what we see today, and try to be critical of that.

Then, on top of that is the discourse between post-colonialism, which is a more rational framing of how we think about our professions, because there are these typologies that emerge through colonisation. So when you think about plazas, streets, squares, gardens – all of those are typologies. You can go back to the centuriation by the Romans, the first thing they did was put in the two streets (*decumanus maximus* and *cardo maximus*) because that's a way of claiming landscape. And so once you're able to critique that – whether you go to One Mile Square or any sprawling, grassy park in Australia – that's a colonial move to claim a landscape. That's a disempowering of native people. The Romans were really good at it, because they showed this kind of formal power of the landscape that then relegated local tradition.

Then are these more informal hybrids. These are things that come through a vernacular relationship with the landscape, and language then becomes really important. So, if I don't call something a park, I don't call it a plaza, I don't call it a street, I don't call it a square, I don't use those kinds of more imperial or colonial terminologies, then I have to find a new vernacular for it, and cultures do that in places. They will call a place Brookdale, they'll say Tree Top, they'll say Echo Glen, and those relate specifically to places. A glen is a clearing, Brookdale because there was water. But when we become attuned to that, we can ... begin to move into a new way of thinking.

The book then takes projects where I've tried to be transgressive – where those typologies exist and I'm pushing against them – versus these new things that we've made like the Solar Strand at the University of Buffalo.

An example of a hybrid I showed today might be the grove of olive trees at The Broad museum in Los Angeles. Just a grove of trees, it's not a plaza. And it's that notion that a grove of trees can exist in this space, without it becoming a plaza. Because once it becomes a plaza then there's an expectation of what you should do with it, and who can be in it. But a grove – you could have fairies – you could have all kinds of things.

In addition to the interview, *Kerb* attended Hood's presentation at the conference:

Hood's work is quite political, while still maintaining what people would consider to be the core outputs of landscape architects. His approach is encapsulated in his talk about a recent project at Princeton University and the memorialisation of Woodrow Wilson:

WH: I do think we have to hold people accountable and we shouldn't be afraid to call people out. This is a piece that's going to be in Princeton. And it's about this guy, twenty-eighth President of the United States, Woodrow Wilson. He's an interesting man. He's from the South like I am; I'm from North Carolina, he's from South Carolina. He went on to become President, I didn't.

WEB Du Bois had this notion of this idea of 'twoness' and he talks about the American Negro having 'two thoughts, two unreconciled strivings; two warring ideals in one dark body, whose strength alone keeps it from being torn asunder'. He talks about this 'longing to obtain conscious manhood, to merge his double self into a better and truer self'. And I've been having this running argument, with colleagues, that we're better and truer ourselves today, that we're resilient because we're still here 100 years later. I'm not burdened by being able to talk to you guys, but maybe my grandfather was, that he had to figure out how to talk to you guys. Right, I'm not burdened by that, I'm educated, I actually teach you guys. So this notion of the 'double consciousness' is no longer a burden for a lot of people of colour now. I'll also argue for women that we've had to deal with this condition.

There's a privileged group of people that never have to think about the double. They never have to think about, 'oh people are not looking at me any different'. And so I chose to call out Woodrow Wilson through this idea. Could I, on this campus of Princeton, his Princeton, really call him into question? So that, when people come to the site – to this hallowed place – they have a way to critique this white man. In this context of the *Fountain of Freedom* – this place where people leave gifts, this beautiful building by Yamasaki – could I make his legacy feel that burden?

The first movement was this: we had two columns – we created polemic – one black, one white. I just presented this in Princeton and an alumnus came up and he said, 'Wow, you really make Wilson kneel'. And I had never thought about that, but he's a broken man, through

this kind of metaphor. And then we bring issues of segregation, of oriental colonialism, of Ku Klux Klan, racism, of his treatment of women, all of these things to the forefront, in a very simple design – which is a square cut in half – that opens his guts up to us. We can now see him and critique him in a very different way.

It's a forty-foot-tall piece, located in Scudder Plaza; all the students pass through this space. It spires up to the sky, so on the one hand you might think it's a monument, but in a way it's an anti-monument. As you move around the landscape [you see] its curations about education, labour, role of government, women's suffrage, relations and segregation. Wilson did some amazing things, modern day education we owe to Woodrow Wilson, but he also segregated government. There were African Americans, there were free black slaves who had high positions. He took their jobs away in 1913 and made them postal carriers. Some of them quit. On the outside, the epitaph, we've gone through all of his writings; sometimes he talks in great heights and sometimes in great lows. But we wanted those images and those words to not be edited. It's a stone glass which is highly reflective and the words again will be unedited. And what I mean by unedited, we're not looking to make something happy or something sad, we're trying to sort of put his words together so that you can kind of see the complexity, but you can also see, right, that it's not neutral in any way. And the last piece we used lenticular printing. We found one of the last lenticular artists in Boston, he's working with us to create this forced, staged lenticular, where the prints are printed on these ribs, so that as you move by you get these four images moving.

And all of his detractors, everyone from Trotter, WEB Du Bois, Susan B Anthony, they're all there telling him, 'why are you doing this to us', 'you must answer to us'. They called out his issues on lynching, they called him out on segregation, they called him out on many things. But he was privileged, he could just keep going.

This piece will be erected this fall, so if you're in Princeton it should be there. And like the other pieces, again, we don't see this as "spectacle"; it's intentional that it's kind of hidden in the grove, but it's something hopefully that you will come upon. And as you walk inside, one side is stainless steel with the quotes and the other side is lenticular. So you're kind of trapped, right within Wilson's inner being.

Sarah Dooling

GREEN GENTRIFICATION & EQUITY

The design fields have conventionally touted the economic benefits of projects, including green infrastructure projects, while only recently recognising how they contribute to creating economic hardships for vulnerable residents.[1] The dynamics of green-gentrification projects that improve the environmental and social conditions of a place but subsequently displace the original residents, raise urgent, uncomfortable questions.

How will design work improve environmental conditions given the realities of widening income disparities and climate-related impacts? How might design projects avoid the zero-sum game attributed so often to the "green up – pricing out" dynamic in under-invested neighbourhoods? What obligations do designers have when it comes to making places that are dynamic and resilient?

This work is a product of a graduate student design studio that foregrounded equity in the pursuit of designing for climate resilience.

Climate resilience in a gentrifying neighbourhood in Austin, Texas

In 2016, the City of Austin's Office of Sustainability contracted with a graduate-level planning and design studio at the University of Texas at Austin. The goal was to develop a climate resilience plan for the year 2050, complete with design prototypes, for a vulnerable neighbourhood in Austin.

The students conducted a city-wide vulnerability assessment, compiling data related to flood risk, urban heat island measures, impervious cover, public green spaces, annual median income and households below poverty line, educational attainment, high school graduation rates, neighbourhood amenities (e.g. public transit lines, grocery stores, public schools) and changes in home sale prices and demographics as measures of gentrification pressures. The east Austin neighbourhood, known as MLK-183, emerged as the neighbourhood with a powerful combination of social and environmental vulnerabilities.

Named after the intersection of East Martin Luther King Boulevard and Highway 183, this neighbourhood contains higher concentrations of industrial and polluting land uses, less canopy cover and poorer quality housing stock compared to the rest of the city. The public schools are underperforming. There are limited commercial areas, no grocery store and no medical clinic. Thirty-two per cent of the people live below the poverty line. Forty-seven per cent of individuals are not educated beyond high school, and only nine per cent have a college degree. Historically, African Americans constituted the

Making design relevant in a segregated world

majority, and now Hispanics are moving in as African American households are leaving.

The fencing off of creeks and large tracts of contaminated parcels of land are part of the legacies of racial policies and lax land use regulations. There are two urban creeks, which have been paved and fenced off. Inaccessible to residents and lacking diverse riparian communities, the creeks have become as much a hazard as a benefit, contributing to flooding and urban heat island issues during the Texas summers. The neighbourhood has a relatively high proportion of vacant land (close to twenty-five per cent), in addition to a relatively low number of street trees. The themes of inaccessibility and hostility became a focal point for the students in thinking about the development of this neighbourhood as an outgrowth of decisions made within relations of power, class and economics.

The Office of Sustainability originally considered resilience the ability of the neighbourhood to bounce back from the stressors and harms caused by heat stress, flooding and drought. Resilience is about building capacity in landscapes – for carbon sequestration, water filtration and photosynthesis – and also in the systems that can transform the lives of residents – including educational, civic, health and justice systems. Through conversations with students, the Office of Sustainability agreed to make equity the central organising principle for developing strategies supportive of resilience, because of the historical legacies of Austin's 1928 plan which designated east Austin as a 'Negro District'.

Using the language of resource efficiency, city politicians argued that concentrating the segregated forms of infrastructure provided fiscal efficiency, implying that such segregationist plans were part of good governance. Following the 1928 plan, east Austin neighbourhoods became places where the city underinvested in public infrastructure, and where industrial land uses proliferated, exposing residents to contaminated lands and polluted waterways. In spite of these hardships, east Austin became the cultural heart for African Americans, with active faith-based communities and music establishments. For the students, after reflecting on the implications of the 1928 plan, equity was defined as access to environmental, economic and cultural opportunities.

The primary goal of the recommendations was to reduce the vulnerability of neighbourhood households to flood risk, water scarcity and extreme heat by increasing their capacity to cope and thrive in an uncertain but more positive future. Students anticipated that residents

Artwork by Carolina Catrola

and business owners would focus on flooding issues and trying to stay cool in the extreme heat of summer. Education emerged as the key strategy, as identified by participants, for empowering and inspiring residents about a more positive future.

The other main concerns identified were: high rates of incarceration among youth (the school-to-prison pipeline); the re-entry of formerly incarcerated adults; socially isolated elders and single parent households; housing unaffordability; and a prevalence of alienation from city government. Each proposed recommendation focused on changing the imbalance of power in order to improve access to opportunities. Social issues are the starting point through which to engage environmental issues, thus they became core to our proposals.

The first proposal called for establishing an educational program that partnered youth with city-employed biologists, ecologists, hydrological engineers and landscape architects. The goal of the Urban Ecology Neighbourhood Collective was to connect city scientists with local public school students through an apprenticeship program focused on projects related to urban hydrology, urban forestry and green infrastructure. Neighbourhood public school teachers would partner with city scientists to train students in technical skills related to green infrastructure design and maintenance.

The second recommendation built on existing programs in public schools that partner adults and youth with mentors. The aim of these programs is to develop communities of caring and healing as a first step in reversing youth alienation and depression, stemming the rates of incarceration, and promoting mental and physical health in poor, psychologically stressed families. A Social Health Network was proposed, which involved expanding the number of restorative justice coordinators. Restorative justice involves educators, youth and families working with a network of mentors and advocates, substituting jail time with community service projects. Students also proposed expanding the existing network of health care practitioners who work in the neighbourhood, connecting people to doctors and navigating public health insurance systems. With no hospital or medical clinic in this neighbourhood, several people shared how disconnected and alienated residents can feel in trying to find health care information and providers. Community health workers also help people exiting the criminal system to re-enter community life by providing assistance with finding employment and housing.

The Learning Landscape Program was intended to improve environmental conditions while providing educational opportunities for residents of all ages. The students proposed using vacant land to establish experiments for growing food, and design strategies focused on reducing flood risk and creating more shade. The ownership of these parcels could be assumed by churches, many of which have gardens, and neighbourhood public schools, whose grounds are fenced off, denying community access.

The last proposal addressed the housing affordability and gentrification crisis. Funding and maintaining affordable housing in Texas is difficult due to constraints outlined in the state constitution which limit restrictions that can legally be placed on private property's ability to generate tax revenues. This, in turn, limits long-term affordability of homes. Local municipalities cannot mandate the production of affordable housing units from developers – this constraint also hinders the production of low-income housing. A common strategy for producing low-income affordable housing in Texas involves establishing community land trusts which use a renewable ninety-nine-year ground lease to ensure long-term affordability. All the units built on the community land trust remain affordable for the life of the trust.

The proposed Community Infrastructure Investment Corporation would be able to secure government funds for affordable home production, and then to use these funds as assets in creating business partnerships with developers. Community Investment Infrastructure Corporations already exist in the United States, receiving government funding for infrastructural projects related to energy. The students also proposed a community land trust, involving the local non-profit affordable housing builder and funded by grants obtained from the Community Infrastructure Investment Corporation, as the initial strategy to increasing the units of affordable housing.

Design for a segregated world

In this studio, design students assumed the obligation to the people made vulnerable both directly via speculative development and indirectly via environmental improvements. The histories of investment, disinvestment and exclusionary practices are important for discerning how economic forces have shaped land uses, regulations and cultural expressions. Without this historical background, the students would not have been able to accurately and compassionately integrate different perceptions of risk between residents and city staff. Nor would they have been able to develop strategies with the potential for repair and healing. For creating designs able to respond to histories of exclusion and segregation, knowing a community's history is fundamental to good practice.

The scope of design work needed to effectively create possibilities for social and ecological resilience is far bigger than conventional site scale. We learned that scaling up is necessary in order to integrate the systems that have co-evolved in maintaining inequities. When equity is prioritised, resilience involves building capacity in the educational, civic, health and justice systems to support educated, politically engaged, healthy, free residents.

Education, stable and safe housing and social networks are fundamental determinants for human health, as is access to green space. The language of health avoids the rhetorical bind that green gentrification presents: poor people versus nature. While the realities of urban economics cannot be denied, designers must become savvy storytellers about building healthy landscapes and healthy communities, thereby inviting collaborations and possibilities for green, vibrant futures for all residents – our human and non-human neighbours.

Yazid Ninsalam & Michaela Prescott

THE WHITE ELEPHANT AND THE FOREST CITY

Reclamation for island one of four began in 2015 and ended in 2018. Topside development will continue till 2025. (Google Earth Pro 7.3.2.5776, 64-bit, (11 November 2018). Forest City Island 1, Gelang Patah, Malaysia. 1°20'20.48"N, 103°35'37.60"E, Eye alt 5.4 km DigitalGlobe 2019)

1 km

Selective perception is the process by which individuals perceive what they want to while disregarding viewpoints at odds with their own. Broadly, it identifies the way in which people have a tendency to "see things" based on their particular frame of reference. In this article, we explore selective perception in the context of infrastructural projects within rapidly developing economies. We discuss a range of ways of seeing China's One Belt, One Road policy, which on the one hand is heralded as a pathway to connectivity, higher speed and shared prosperity in global trade, yet on the other is criticised as an attempt to build China's political influence at the expense of poorer nations. This sets the backdrop for re-perceiving the conception and delivery of the Forest City development in Malaysia.

One Belt One Road

The ripple effect of Chinese President Xi Jinping's 2013 key foreign policy One Belt, One Road should not be understated. The policy now commonly known as the Belt and Road Initiative (BRI) spans more than sixty-five countries that account collectively for over thirty per cent of global gross domestic product, sixty-two per cent of the global population, and seventy-five per cent of known energy reserves. Under this policy China underwrites billions of dollars of infrastructure investments to improve regional cooperation and connectivity on a trans-continental scale.[1] In essence, the initiative is a collection of interlinking trade deals and infrastructure projects throughout Eurasia and the Pacific. However, the definition of what exactly qualifies as a BRI project or which countries are even involved in the initiative is still unclear.

The initiative consists of two parts and builds on existing land and maritime passages, namely the Silk Road Economic Belt and the 21st Century Maritime Silk Road. On land, a host of trade and infrastructure projects are articulated along roads stretching from China to Europe. At sea, a network of shipping lanes and port developments is placed strategically throughout Asia and the Pacific. To meet this ambitious expansion across land and sea, China, with the support of the partner countries, is technically redrawing the map for global trade and claiming ground through the strategic installation of terrestrial and marine infrastructure.

White elephants

The implications of large infrastructure projects on participating nations continue to draw opposing views, with praise from the East and flak from the West, both sides understanding the intention of the initiative differently. China's Foreign Minister, Wang Yi, maintains that the BRI is not a 'geostrategic concept' but is part of efforts to build 'a community with a shared future for mankind together with countries around the globe'.[2] Participating nations welcome financial support to relieve the infrastructural stress demanded of a rapidly developing economy. However, despite the program's purportedly altruistic aims, this aid brings with it relatively high interest rates and lending volumes that result in some countries being at particular risk of debt distress.[3]

The manicured gardens on island 1 of the Forest City development lack the ecological richness of the land- and seascapes they have replaced.

In 2017, after Sri Lanka defaulted on development loans from the program, its strategic port of Hambantota was handed over to state-controlled China Merchants Port Holdings Company. Naysayers cite this as a cautionary tale, evidenced by the ninety-nine-year handover agreement that includes a seventy per cent stake in the harbour and 15,000 acres of land. Unfortunately, predictions of 100,000 new jobs over three to five years from the original proponents of the port project failed to materialise.[4]

In an article titled 'Just what is this One Belt, One Road thing anyway?' CNN cites Jörg Wuttke of the EU Chamber of Commerce in China, who expressed concerns that the initiative has increasingly 'been hijacked by Chinese companies, which have used it as an excuse to evade capital controls, smuggling money out of the country by disguising it as international investments and partnerships'.[5] Wuttke further warns that the BRI is unregulated, and key infrastructure projects carried out under its brand have failed to live up to expectations, becoming a 'huge white elephant that left an enormous amount of wasted resources strewn along its path'.[6]

Forest City

The Forest City project in Johor, Malaysia, sits on four human-made islands and once completed will house over 700,000 people on 1386 hectares, an area ten times the size of Melbourne's Hoddle Grid. With the project master plan designed by Sasaki, a multidisciplinary design firm based out of Boston and Shanghai, the development is set to be Southeast Asia's most extensive mixed-use green development.[7] The master plan sought to protect the area's delicate seagrass ecosystem, which is relied upon by the local fishing industry, and reinforce this by re-establishing mangroves, coves and mudflats. The master plan was recognised in 2016 with a Merit Award for Analysis and Planning by the Boston Society of Landscape Architects.

On the regional scale, the project strategically straddles the Special Economic Zone of Iskandar, Malaysia, and the island nation Singapore. It is the result of a sixty/forty joint venture between two property development companies, the Hong Kong-listed Country Garden Holdings Ltd (CG) and Malaysian company Esplanade Danga 88 Sdn Bhd, which is state-owned. Within the context of the Maritime Silk Road, it lies between the upcoming Kuantan deepwater port and industrial park to the east, and the Melaka Gateway project to the west. This project continues the network of shipping lanes and port developments along the Maritime Silk Road and establishes China's presence in the Southeast Asia maritime trade routes. At the local scale, the project is adjacent to the port of Tanjung Pelepas in south-western Johor and north-west of Singapore.

In a 2014 Detailed Environmental Impact Assessment (DEIA), Forest City is described as follows: '[a] development that centres on wellness by emphasising a lifestyle that is harmonic and healthy, in a sustainable environment and in an urban setting that is efficient and comfortable to live, work and study in, and for recreation.'[8] In such a land-rich region, it is difficult to comprehend how this necessitates the creation of four new islands, to be constructed through a process of land reclamation, dredging works and topside development over the next three decades.

At the present rate of development, despite adhering to the mitigation measures published in the DEIA, the local fishing industry has expressed concerns over the reclamation and dredging work which has degraded the seagrass bed causing loss of fishing grounds.[9] The failure of the current local economy seems a high price to pay in exchange for the outlook of future rapid economic growth, in particular given the unfulfilled promise of a bustling Hambantota Port.

Furthermore, locals have expressed worries that they cannot afford property within the development and are anxious about how the government will integrate the influx of international buyers.[10] Conversely, prospective Chinese buyers who have been wooed by the developers are disadvantaged by the mainland's tightened capital controls for overseas purchasers, which have seen them unable to follow through on payments after the initial deposit is in.[11] Although Malaysian Prime Minister Mahathir bin Mohamed has capped foreigners from buying further residential units, this has not been received well by the developer who is struggling with faltering demand.[12]

Although Forest City is not part of the chain of state-led BRI projects, it is demonstrably aligning itself to the same 'New Silk Road' hype, with a map of Eurasia and Africa pointing to Forest City's 'strategic location' amidst Beijing's winding BRI trade routes filling a wall within its sales office.[13] While the ongoing construction of Forest City is steeped in controversy[14], the developers continue to use the original master plan's accolades to attract potential investors with the rhetoric of a better, more sustainable tomorrow. It seems unlikely that the green skyscrapers of Forest City will justify the environmental and socio-economic displacement of the existing community, and the destruction of its marine and terrestrial environments.

Conclusion

Whether it is focused on the greater geostrategic intention of these initiatives or evaluating the possible effects of participating in the BRI for individual countries, the discussion of the merit of the BRI and its spin-offs continues. By framing the Forest City project in the broader regional development context of the BRI, we have shown how selective perception can play out across scales and how different stakeholders have used the policy – sometimes at the expense of others – to achieve their own goals. Reflecting on these case studies has presented a window on patterns of influence in development politics at a global and regional scale.

Roberto Boettger

S T E P S

PROPOSAL FOR RECLAIMING THE MOUNTAINS OF RIO DE JANEIRO

Diagram:
The Mountain as a Project

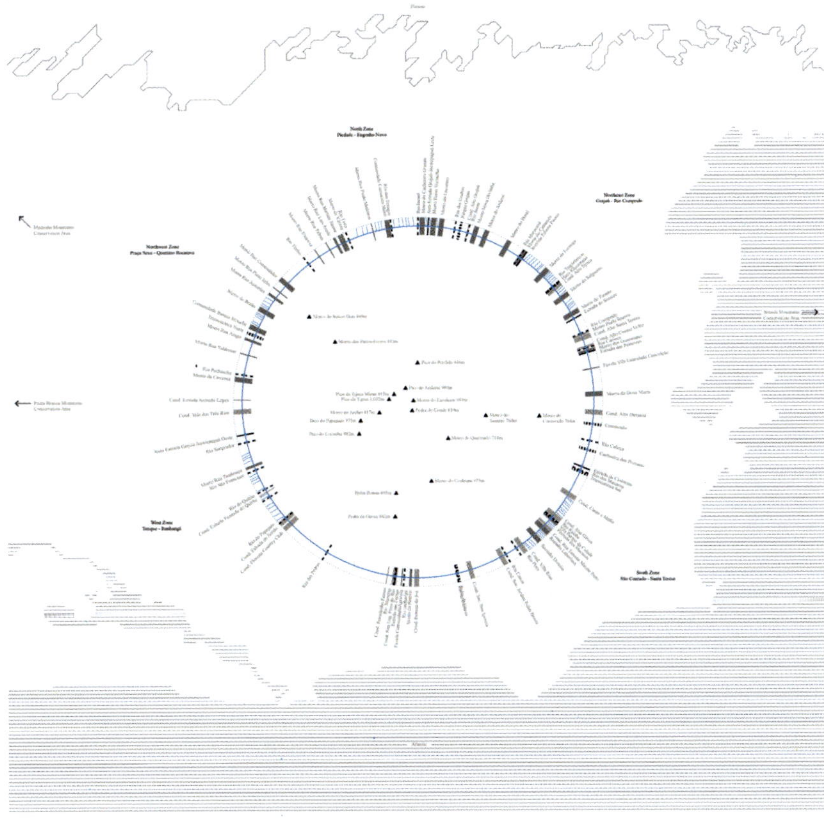

This project addresses the enclosure of unbuilt land in conservation areas as a device that shapes a territory beyond its given environmental policies. It situates itself within the metropolitan region of Rio de Janeiro, Brazil, where enclosed mountains shape the city socially and politically like no other force. These have, on one hand, provided a green backdrop to the city and served as a juridical instrument capable of keeping developers from building on the land. They have also, on the other hand, served as a device for land appropriation that keeps the rhetoric of access through tourism but that ultimately creates the separation of dwelling, of experience. The project proposes a network of paths, stairs and terraces that enable access to and use of the forested hillsides.

In reality, that which is being tamed into the glass box of the nature reserve is anything but natural. Before the Portuguese arrived in the sixteenth century, the mountain was used as a commons for the native peoples. A grid was then laid over the mountain by the sesmarias system of land distribution for the colonisation of the territory. Cultivation reached its climax when plantation owners found in the hillsides the perfect condition for the coffee tree. In the post-independence, mid-nineteenth century, the plantations were disappropriated and the hillsides were reforested. Some of the land was further designed into public parks. Despite its apparent "naturalness", the mountain today conceals a "calculated totality" which has effectively erased its past iterations.

Throughout the twentieth century, it was gradually enclosed into a mosaic of UNESCO, national, state and municipal conservation areas. These have appeared as the natural way of managing unbuilt land so that all citizens - including the lower class - seem to benefit from their implementation. Their political agency, however, becomes apparent when a narrative is constructed to dictate what is to be included or excluded.

Territorial Strategy:
Metropolitan Rio de Janeiro

Such control of the landscape, by rendering the mountain "untouchable", sublimates processes of separation.[1]

It is thus proposed that a system of stairs continue the city street grid into the human-made rainforest, up to a footpath that follows an existing legal boundary at the 100-metre-elevation contour line. This divides the land into plots that are to be managed by local, collective stakeholders – a continuous process of negotiation into decentralising management. These stakeholders may include universities, schools, hospitals and community centres. The strategy is complemented by existing hiking trails, roads, rivers and urbanisation that intersect with the boundary.

Aligned with the steps and paths are structures that facilitate the use of the forested hillsides. The archetype of the *terreiro* – or 'sorting ground' from coffee plantations preceding the current forest – enables and legitimises the ritual of foraging activities. *Terreiros* were simply flattened terraces with markings on the ground that suggested a methodology for sorting harvested produce.

Urban Scale:
Tijuca Mountain

Since colonial times, moreover, *terreiros* have become emancipatory spaces for social and cultural gatherings that remain to this day a part of Brazilian society. They are complemented by additional structures such as collective toolsheds, resting areas, water fountains, emergency facilities and viewing points. Although these elements are precise in what they do their sheer abstraction as landscape mediation lends them to other uses.

Despite its minimal levels of intervention, the project accommodates the scale of the territory. It provides a new sense of orientation to the city that allows a reading of the mountain not only as a natural but as a collective space. The relationship between enclosed landscape and city becomes a possibility once again. The mountain thus reveals itself for what it really is: a designed artefact. The notion of "museification"[2] is profanated by its very own rules, where the act of preserving is also the act of using.

Ed Kermode & Dan Parker

A 3D-scanned tree isolated from its surrounds.
Image: Dan Parker and Alex Holland (2018).

NONHUMAN STAKEHOLDERS

Urban inequity and nonhuman exclusivity

Under global neoliberal policies and planning mechanisms, social systems are becoming increasingly structurally violent towards much of the population in favour of the hyper-wealthy few. Widening inequity can be attributed to the hegemony of neoliberal thought and governance that is associated with deregulation of the market and ambitions of greater individual economic freedoms.

As a product of neoliberal knowledge, contemporary cities are being aggregately spatialised by 'zones of exclusion' as vehicles to maintain social and environmental privileges for a select few. Murray's[1] in-depth investigation of contemporary urbanisation describes zones of exclusion as denoting 'a hardening of the borders and boundaries that separate, divide, and fragment urban space'. These urban enclaves, such as gated housing communities in Cape Town or multiuse complexes in Istanbul, are the products of global neoliberal forces in which capital and power are spatialised as fragments within urban landscapes.

Global urbanism, assemblage urbanism, enclave urbanism, aggregate urbanism – these terms are increasingly gaining traction, in both architectural and geographical literature, to describe contemporary urbanisation. While these urban theories have extensively commented on the marginalisation of certain human communities, less attention has been given to the exclusion of nonhuman agencies from city-making processes. In an era of unprecedented habitat loss, species extinction, climate change and ecosystem collapse, there is an acute need to design cities for nonhuman organisms. However, nonhumans are often overlooked in design processes, whereby their capacity to act independently and help shape the environments they are situated within (i.e. "agency") is rarely acknowledged. How then can design professions better acknowledge nonhuman agency within overarching neoliberal structures that are arguably out of reach to change? By viewing the problem via a biopolitical framework, this article aims not only to understand the mechanisms that underpin exclusive urban development, but also to offer a possible approach to include nonhumans as stakeholders within design processes. Using trees as a case study, firstly this article looks at how nonhuman beings are represented in existing neoliberal discourses, before speculating on alternative ways of acknowledging nonhuman agency within design processes.

Biopolitics and nonhuman commodification

Interpreting the contemporary city using a biopolitical lens enables the dissection of the intangible forces that create urban zones of exclusion. A Foucauldian biopolitical framework is particularly useful to begin describing and identifying how the uneven distribution of power and resources are spatialised through urban landscapes. Under Foucault's notion of biopolitics, life is subjugated by disciplinary mechanisms of power through the production of capitalist knowledge.[2] It refers to developments whereby the right to seize, repress and destroy life is complemented by a form of power that aims to develop, optimise, order and secure life.[3] When neoliberal capitalist rationality is seen through Foucault's biopolitical lens, life is therefore controlled and regulated to facilitate economic development.

Within the current neoliberal episteme, everything (including "nature" and the environment) is commodified according to its productive economic value to the market. This is problematic as it raises the temptation for urban developers to focus on minimising financial costs, which can consequently lead to detrimental effects on nonhuman stakeholders. Through a biopolitical analysis, where spatiality is defined by those with capital, urban environments become less hospitable to nonhuman agencies that do not carry high economic value. In such developments, nonhumans become viewed as commodities, service providers, objects, property or resources. For example, carbon offset regimes in New York ironically position trees as commodities to alleviate human-made ecological degradation. In this example, the biological functions of 678,183 street trees currently provide US$109,625,536.06 in 'environmental services' per year.[4] Here, the value of trees is quantified and reduced to a monetary figure; a tradeable asset that can be pawned as economic or political agents.

How can design professionals think of other ways to relate to trees that recognises them as agents in the city rather than commodities? Arguably, trees are already valued by people in a myriad of ways for aesthetic, ecological, heritage, symbolic or cultural reasons. Despite this, it is difficult for these views to gain traction in design processes within existing neoliberal structures that monetise the environment.

Digital trees and nonhumans inclusivity

In order to adequately represent nonhuman agency within design processes, there is a need for new ways of perceiving trees not as inanimate commodities but as "actants" with needs and preferences. However, traditional modes of representation within landscape architecture practice struggle to represent nonhumans as actants. For example, the conventional 2D representation of trees in plan and elevation, which are repetitively drawn as flat surfaces bounded by lines, fails to embody the temporal and complex attributes inherent in each individual tree. This section looks at how *digital trees*, captured via 3D scanning techniques, might offer alternative mechanisms for design professionals to consider trees as multiplicitous beings beyond their typically ascribed capital value.

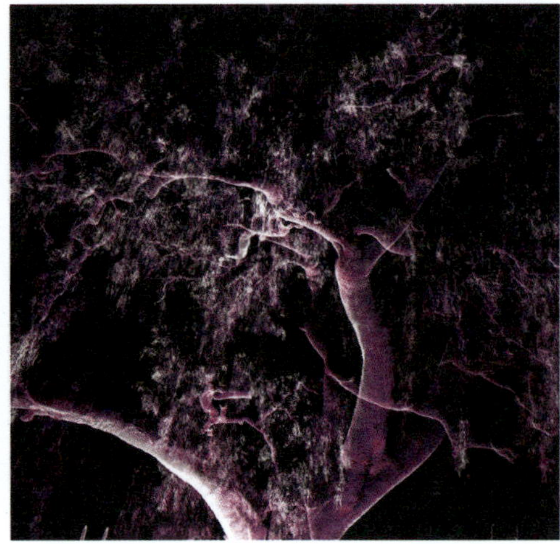

By challenging conventional drawing methods, 3D scanning moves away from the constraints of 2D representation towards point clouds that can better capture the complex qualities of trees. One way this can be done is to isolate the tree from its context such that trees are perceived as individual subjects, each with their own unique form and characteristics in space, rather than objects that are sometimes lost within a homogenous imagery of the 'environment'. Image scanning also offers a way of deconstructing trees into an assemblage of points where each point can be ascribed quantities and values that begin to better represent the multitude of characteristics a tree holds. Rather than a monetary figure, the tree can start to be described with quantitative factors such as light and shade, wind, strength, height, orientation, position, material, surface texture, structure and form. This information can be fed into design processes as parameters that help to create a new set of conditions in the design space, thereby considering aspects of the trees' inclinations that might otherwise go unnoticed. Here the tree becomes positioned as a valued stakeholder that can be integrated within design briefs.

Given that a site may have hundreds, if not thousands, of individual nonhuman species, it may seem unfeasible to analyse every single organism as a stakeholder. However, combining 3D scanning techniques with algorithmic modelling enables the streamlined observation and recording of multiple entities, which would be inconceivable using traditional techniques such as drawing or photos.

Digital trees and nonhuman representation

In addition to quantifying aspects of the trees' characteristics, there is a need for novel and qualitative ways of visually representing the agency of trees. However, it is a difficult task to imagine and depict agency in entities that are not typically considered as individual actants. Trotter[5] eloquently encapsulates how such concerns might enter design processes as important enquiries into possible alternative futures:

> How can we add a bit of agency to those things, and how can we motivate them to keep acting on our behalves, to then also turn around and motivate us... how can we inject imagination into them in such a way that they also inject imagination back into what we believe is possible and actable... I think one of those ways is to create moments of lags... dissonance... as soft as syncopation, but let's say things that are not aligning precisely... that suggest the possibility of other systems, or other organizations, that have yet to be brought into the existing system of things.

In the case of digital trees, can the use of certain representational techniques inject agency into nonhuman life forms that can then motivate design professionals to act on that agency? Drawing on Trotter's speculation, the inaccuracies of the scans should be recognised and embraced in a way that depicts their unique characteristics. For example, the images contain overlapping points, or 'glitches', that are hangovers from the capturing techniques which involve combining multiple different scans from different angles. When this misalignment is compounded with varying scales, colour, angles and perspectives, it is possible to start depicting ideas of temporality, fragility and need for support. Can 3D scanning then serve as a catalyst to produce new forms of knowledge on nonhuman agency within the design profession?

If knowledge is understood as being reproduced through power, when analysed under a biopolitical lens, then these explorations of representations can be seen as offering a platform to begin challenging the naturalised logic of neoliberalism, which commodifies the environment. While the terms biopolitics, neoliberalism and assemblage urbanism can be interpreted in many ways, it is exactly the blurriness of the concepts that makes them productive. Not only can these frameworks help to better understand the processes underpinning structural inequities for both human and nonhuman beings, it can be used to productively reinterpret design approaches.

This article recognises the difficulty of changing these structures, but speculates on alternative mechanisms by which nonhuman agency can be better considered within hegemonic neoliberal operations. While relatively nascent in design professions, 3D scanning provides new ways of seeing, interpreting and valuing nonhuman entities as individual stakeholders worthy of attention and respect.

A 3D-scanned tree in perspective view.
Image: Dan Parker and Alex Holland
(2018).

The Pigeon Paradox: perception and the urban non-human

The urban assemblage contains many more actors than are factored in the design equation. Selective perception can blind designers to social groups but can also obscure the diverse non-human world that coinhabits our cities.

As an ontological framework, assemblage theory can be used to break down physical, temporal and territorial borders in social systems; to see them as fluid, complex and relational. However, the urban assemblage does not end at the social or human.[1]

An abundance of non-human actors live alongside us, beneath us, inside us, often finding habitat in the cracks, ruin and forgotten places in our cities. As they scurry through sewers, echolocate fruit trees, release spores into the wind or sit obediently like a good dog, the city environment shapes their lives as starkly as it does our own.

This essay aims to shine a light on the diverse but obscured urban non-human assemblage and investigate how design might better comprehend and include the non-human world.

Conceptual / geographical placement

The language we use to mark and understand non-humans has spatial consequences; discourse informs design. The conceptual placement of non-humans affects their geographical placement, inclusion or exclusion.[2] A critical interrogation of these conceptual placements reveals a complex assemblage, with implications for power, agency and inclusion.

Categorisation of the non-human

Current discourse tends to categorise non-human urban actors as nature, domestic or pest. These rigid categories lead to some actors being designed in, while many are intentionally or inadvertently designed out. Interrogating these three categories reveals unexpected relationships, complexities and systems tangled up in the urban assemblage.

Nature has always been a complex and contested categorisation. Ecofeminists argue that nature is socially constructed along a Cartesian binary - on one side is human / designed / rational and on the other nature / untouched / irrational.[3] This makes nature in the city paradoxical.[4] Urban nature is often described as: remnant, regenerated, revegetated and restored. Each of these terms construct nature as opposed to the city and imply that nature is held in the past, a relic, static.[5] Design that brings nature into the city is often positioned as an attempt to remedy the city. Design intervention removes the perception of environment as natural, and so designers aim for a naturalistic aesthetic. This way of thinking can lead us to undervalue ecologies that do not appear naturalistic.[6] For example, the Werribee Water Treatment Plant, despite huge ecological richness is not always acknowledged in the same way as a more picturesque

---

Bede Brennan & Minna Leunig

THE PLACES YOU END UP

ecology.[7] But not all urban non-humans are afforded the status of nature.

Domestic non-humans, cultivated and tamed, are designed into the city. Pets, ornamental plants, lawns, livestock and other domestic non-humans are an edited incarnation of their ancestors, shaped by human preference to fit within human places. They are designed in, not just in the form of dog parks and elm avenues, but in the design of resource flows. Pets are sustained on a diet of imported meats from anonymous creatures in shadow places.[8] Ornamental trees are kept alive with scarce water, diverted towards the city. The domestic is supported by a broader human altered ecology. The metabolism of our cities is designed to support these domestic non-humans in the same way it supports humans.

The third category are pests; weeds, vermin and non-humans deemed undesirable. The development of unbalanced, disturbed ecological mosaics in our cities makes pest creatures inevitable. Urban pest creatures emerge to fill ecological gaps, finding habitat in unintentional spaces and systems beneath the surface of what has been designed. Fattened on wasted food, supplied with runoff nutrients, or pioneered in disturbed soil, pest non-humans become the target of herbicides, traps and eradication programs. Including these groups into the design equation, rather than reacting to their emergence, could lead to better outcomes.
For example, research into pigeon populations suggests constructing tailored pigeon roosting areas and better managing food waste, keeps populations smaller and healthier, while reducing conflict between humans and pigeons.[9]

Exploration of specific cases shows the categories of nature, domestic and pest are fluid. The pigeons in our city (*Columba livia domestica*) now a pest, all descend from an ancient domestic strain. Flying foxes (*Pteropus mammalia pteropodidae*), an endemic and vulnerable bat species, fit best in the category of nature. But flying foxes are becoming increasingly attracted to the urban environment and as they move into botanic gardens in cities across Australia, they have increasingly become considered a pest.[10] The reliance of flying foxes on the city is seen as a problem; as the climate changes, and cities increasingly suck water and other resources from their surrounds, perhaps urban adaptation is an appropriate strategy.

These socially constructed categories are built around an anthropocentric bias, giving the impression that humans are the sole shapers of these assemblages. Yet human and non-human have shaped each other, both with agency, and so perhaps both shape our cities.

Urban ecology

The emergent field of urban ecology has shown that urban ecosystems are more resilient, rich and globally diverse than once thought.[11] Although city creation undeniably leads to a reduction in species richness, and an increase in introduced species biomass, peri-urban edges often contain higher biodiversity than surrounding rural areas. Globally, cities

contain at least 20 per cent of the avian biodiversity.[12] Melbourne supports six threatened or endangered species, which exist nowhere else in the world.[13] Despite being altered and degraded, urban ecologies are not dead, and are places of hybridity and experimentation.

Umwelten

Some of our misconstruction of the non-human world perhaps comes down to phenomenology; non-humans operate in a different *umwelten* to humans.[14] An *umwelt* is the sensory and perceptual world of an organism. An urban spider, for example, exists in an *umwelten* fundamentally different to ours, perceiving colours, sounds and movements we cannot comprehend. Non-human experiences of urban places don't always sensorially overlap with our own.

Sensing and technology

Technology increasingly shapes our interactions with place. Satellite imagery, Pokémon Go, Light Detection and Ranging (LIDAR), temperature monitoring nodes, and countless others help to build novel, augmented or extended understandings of site. This movement away from 'direct' sensorial experience of site, place or ecology, into data collection and representation, could reinforce marginalisation of non-human worlds not recognised by technologies.

Yet sensing technology presents a possible opportunity. Within assemblage, technology is not separate from, but an extension of the human/technology hybrid.[15] Perhaps the ability to peer into obscured *umwelten*, to understand and map previously imperceptible light frequencies, air movements, and scents, offers a way for our sensory knowledge to better overlap with our non-human housemates.

Some examples from the UK and US show how data and design can intersect with the non-human world to enrich urban ecologies. A combination of simple user generated data from i-tree and ebird in Philadelphia and New York has led to a deeper understanding of complex relationships, and therefore a more evidence-based design approach.[16] Researchers discovered surprising relationships between species and were able to offer improved planting recommendations based on this.

Implications for design

Human wellbeing cannot be separated from urban ecologies, and their effects on us.[17] The past few hundred years (and the colonial project) has seen direct sensorial communication with the non-human world becomes less rich, to the detriment of human wellbeing.[18] One step towards inclusion of urban non-humans is to interrogate and question existing categories, and look at the urban assemblage as a single intertwined metabolism. Perhaps there are also opportunities to use emerging technologies to peek into worlds once obscured to humans. Designers, as the most powerful shapers of this shared urban place, must develop a more nuanced, complex vision of urban non-humans, and recognise their participation in shaping our cities.

Lewis McNeice

N A T U R A L D I S A S T E R S R E S I L I E N C E V U L N E R A B I L I T Y

The increasing size and severity of disasters around the world[1] clearly highlights the consequences of exclusive design deepening structural inequity. It also emphasises the need for design professionals to critically evaluate questions like 'who are we really designing for?'

Three issues immediately come to mind. One, that the question should be amended to 'who are we designing *with*?' as the use of the word *for* brings with it a power dynamic and exacerbates issues of design hierarchies. An example of this can be found following the 2010 Haiti earthquake.

Two, we must include 'within what structures?' As the response to the events surrounding Hurricane Katrina in the US in 2005 attests, if the systems and frameworks are imbalanced, fundamentally biased, and if not firstly redesigned, then despite the design outcomes that emerge, the injustices tearing at the social fabric will remain.

Three, the most important theme underpinning both of the previous issues is dignity. A theme, sadly, some critics consider absent during the recovery after the Black Saturday bushfires in Victoria. In order to be truly empathic, open and accountable, designers must engage, collaborate and operate with dignity. The impacts of these inclusions and changes in design methodology will have lasting effects on design's reach, scope and positive effects in our world.

The power dynamics associated with the idea of designing *for* anyone, instead of *with* them, point to a concerning potential for megalomania. A 2010 earthquake saw Haiti inundated with foreign military personnel and well meaning NGOs, all emboldened by good intentions. But as Ivan Illich once said: 'to hell with good intentions'.

In the subsequent redesigning of the country, all too often the Haitian government and Haitians themselves were left out of the equation to dire consequences, further highlighting historical and continuing power imbalances. One critic, for example, cites the fact that after the US military landed in Haiti, uninvited, and took control of the airport, more than thirty per cent of donated US funds went to sustaining US troops and less than three per cent went to stabilising the democratically elected government of Haiti.[2]

Foreign involvement is not new to Haiti, and some have argued that the lasting effects of colonialism were contributing to the collapse of the built environment. Of course there are many complexities involved, but in my opinion the purposeful weakening of the government and subsequent promotion of raging and unrelenting capitalism gave rise to 'regulation be damned' growth that ignored history, context and geography, and was designed for the people and not with the people. Time and again the US has supported dictators who have little internal support, under the guise of progress. It seems to me that they have a share in the responsibility, but, if driven to action, it must only occur invited and in a collaborative and equitable setting. The very presence of largely US NGOs erodes state structures.

Only full respect, recognition and acceptance of Haiti, its history and culture, and its many contexts and complexities will see Haiti designed *with* and not *for*. The role of designers in this context is to let go of power and control and, instead, help Haiti develop a system where design is not gifted but used as a tool of mutual collaboration and dignified respect. Haitian-driven recovery will require a trade of the traditional intrusive paternalism and pressure from international capitalist systems, for an increasingly collaborative, transparent and equitable assistance from designers and politics alike.

This leads us to the second consideration of 'within what structures?' Using the events surrounding Hurricane Katrina as an example, it was not the hurricane making landfall, nor the subsequent failing of the levees that caused the disaster. The stresses impacting New Orleans, and many other major US cities, created an environment for a social disaster that saw the lower-lying, low income, disproportionally African-American communities hit hardest.[3] That social disaster continued; pre-Katrina racial biases and ongoing institutional arrangements culminated in the effects of the storm and its flooding being overwhelmingly felt by African-American residents, and the failure of the US government to act in a timely fashion.

Social capital was the dominant mediator of New Orleanians' experience of Hurricane Katrina. The poverty, housing, employment and education inequality was stark, and hugely racialised. In the face of Katrina, it meant that those with means to do so (predominantly white Americans) fled the city, and those without (the African American population) were stranded. The racism carried through to post-disaster New Orleans. In what's known as environmental justice, we know there are racial dimensions to what happened before, during and after Hurricane Katrina.

Extreme disparities between rich and poor exist in many major US cities; however, criticisms of the US government response also lie in the inaction and ineptitude that saw many thousands of people unable to leave, and left without help from an unwilling government.

The fact of the matter is – with sea levels expected to rise and increasing global temperatures – all the sea walls, levees and dams in the world won't be able to address the myriad race- and gender-based stresses tearing away at the social fabric of our communities. Design solutions don't mean a damn when, due to biases in the institutions in which we live and work, people are inherently worse off based on race, class or gender.

Finally, the third of our considerations, that the response to disasters must be site-specific and human-focussed. Further, in each case, as in the broader context, there are structural barriers denying such affect. What we must be designing for is dignity for all; this is a truth that will continue to improve designers and their designs. The conditions leading up to and events surrounding Black Saturday were totally unprecedented. They forever changed the way we measure and plan for fire, and even affected our collective consciousness regarding fire in south-eastern Australia.

Today, ten years later, the healing is ongoing. And yet, many criticisms can be found regarding the reconstruction efforts and road to recovery that the town of Marysville, for example, was forced to suffer. Like many communities recovering from such an event, people remained, and the people of Marysville were builders, architects, designers, farmers, business-owners and community members with extensive and intimate knowledge of their town, its history, geography, context and future. Yet, according to many of the community leaders, these were the same people being excluded from the design and implementation of the recovery process. Marysville was subjected to well-meaning, predominantly Melbourne-based architects, builders and designers that were ignorant of the context and landscape of Marysville.

Marysville was exposed to a top-down reconstruction effort that saw politicians and media scramble for the speed and haste of a quick rebuild and the illusion of recovery. Buildings going up don't mean much if the community doesn't want them. There's no dignity in a response that sees Marysville, a town without a basketball team, given a state of the art basketball facility to pay off. Obviously, it has been the recovery and rebuilding effort that is the ongoing disaster in Marysville.[4] This is an example of "Thing Theory" that can be described as focusing on building "things" that merely suggest effort and action.[5] Community-lead recovery is offered as an antidote for these issues, if it focuses on dignity in design.

Bad design isn't just committed in the recovery phase of the disaster management cycle but in all phases; as we problematise resilience, we see the lack of critique of power and patriarchy that intensifies hyper-masculinity and ignores dignity.[6] If we are designing for anyone we are beginning in the wrong spot. If we are designing within a flawed system we are doomed to fail. Design is a verb and it must be synonymous with listening, engaging and collaborating if it is to have any real power in changing current power imbalances. We can clearly see the consequences of responding within these current power imbalances and structural inequalities. And, if we get it wrong and exclusivity in design continues, it means more pain and suffering for those already most vulnerable.

What we need to be designing *for* and *with* is dignity. Designing with people, redesigning the systems in which we live, and designing with dignity is the key to designing with all that we are structurally connected to, both human and non-human.

Artwork by Fotis Rovolis

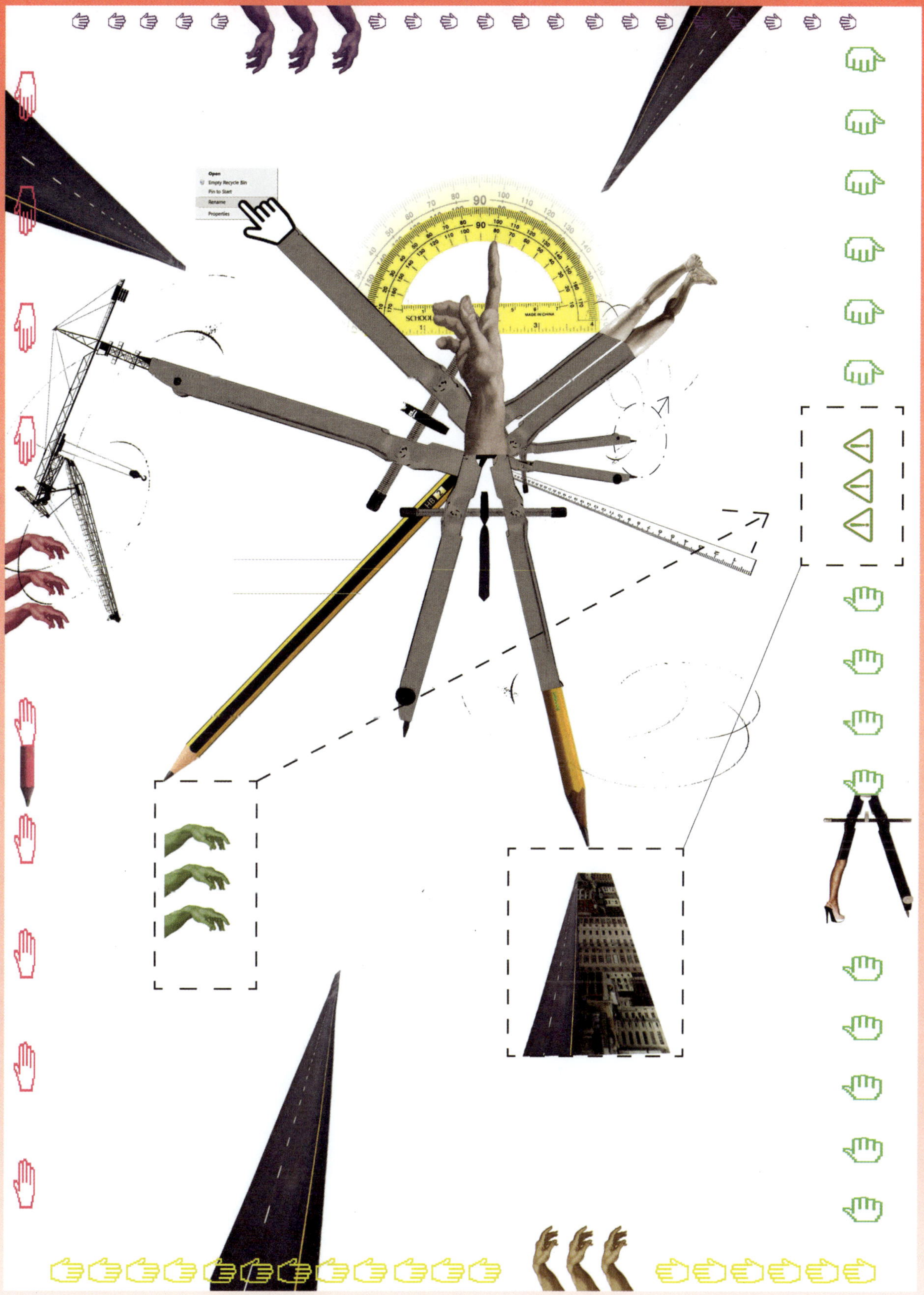

GET UP!

Kate Church

Kate Church attended a joint event held by *Kerb* and TCL.

Billed as an intimate salon, *Get Up! Urban activism and the politics of persuasion* was organised by Ricky Ricardo, the *Kerb* 27 editorial team, and hosted at TCL's Melbourne office. Coinciding with the final days of Australia's 2019 federal election campaign, the event's title doffs its hat to the progressive grassroots independent political movement Get Up! Curated on themes of urban activism, the politics of public space and gender-sensitive design, the event included four designers who expounded on the different forms and modes of public agency; from experimenting with an alternative practice model, to advocating and leading high-profile public campaigns, to developing a 'middle-out' approach that seeks to build gender equity into urban life.

Set-up!

The first presentation was from the co-founders of OFFICE, a not-for-profit multidisciplinary design and research practice. Its purpose is to enhance the agency of design tools and research in order to support and deliver projects with public benefits and an inclusive social and cultural agenda. Steve Mintern and Simon Robinson have determined that to do this with integrity requires alternative governance, legal and operational structures that underpin the practice itself. The frameworks that enable this are notable for their openness. Supporting this set-up is Ampersand, a platform OFFICE has embedded in its practice model, which allows other individuals to plug in and leverage the legitimacy, insurance and the Board of OFFICE on a project-by-project basis.

To date, OFFICE's design dance-card has been relatively full and has already run the gamut of community engagement, master planning, urban design, teaching and research projects. In describing their alternative practice structure, Mintern and Robinson emphasised their focus on experimentation. Their desire to engage with public discourse has fostered a suite of current projects that includes a postgraduate seminar 'Politics of Public Space' where students and members of the wider public gather in public spaces to hear from a diverse range of invited speakers. This lecture series feeds into the way OFFICE positions its work – in response to the perceived deficit and missed opportunities of design disciplines to overtly contribute to public realm discourse. This was highlighted in an anecdote about an earlier project Leftunder. This alternative proposal for Melbourne's level crossing removals saw Robinson and Mintern accused of acting as covert political players. As Robinson noted, 'the fact that people thought it was more likely that we were part of a Labor-funded propaganda machine than design professionals doing their work' reinforced the perception that design is rarely understood as a political act. So don't be fooled by the generic name; OFFICE's approach to the agency of design is anything but.

Speak up!

Against the backdrop of a broader political campaign, which has seen complex issues fought out in soundbites, Tania Davidge's elucidation on the agency of extended conversation with members of the public about design was as refreshing as it was compelling. In calling for people to speak up, Davidge, who collaborates with Christine Phillips as OoPLA, posits that 'politics lies at the intersections of public space and private interests'. She noted that being engaged with a politics of persuasion allows the mode of conversation – of speaking up – to be elevated from an everyday activity to an active strategy that engages the public with their everyday built environments. Indeed, recognising that a 'city is multiple, and the audience is multiple' also necessitates looking at the everyday in a different way. This underpins Glow, a project that uses light to transform existing things, allowing people to see them anew.

As a co-founder of OoPLA (formerly OpenHAUS) much of Davidge's work is concerned with how architecture and the public space is communicated to everyday audiences. She frames architecture as a process as opposed to a built outcome, and is interested in architecture as public, playful and

Get Up! event hosted by *Kerb*.
Image credit Jack Dixon-Gunn.

ACTIVISM THE OF
AND POLITICS PURSUASION

political. These three Ps came into play when Davidge, who is also the president of the public space advocacy group Citizens for Melbourne, ran the successful 'Our City, Our Square' campaign opposing the demolition of Federation Square's Yarra Building and its replacement with an Apple store. Running counter to the predominantly negative media coverage of the built environment, the 'Our City, Our Square' campaign shifted the media narrative, deploying publicity and media releases to create visibility about this issue. Davidge's notion of a 'politics of persuasion' is one of practising design advocacy that invokes speaking up, collaborating and making visible the impact that public space has on our lives.

Step up!

Associate Professor Nicole Kalms was the final speaker and commenced with a discussion about founding the XYX Lab at Monash University's Department of Design. The research lab operates at the intersection of gender, identity, urban space and advocacy. She described the genesis of this lab as wanting to produce research that females were interested in. In particular, female doctoral researchers - and it is their work that directly shapes and feeds into XYX Lab.

Her presentation wove a captivating narrative around the current findings of this research and the extent to which gender shapes an individual's experience and perception of urban space. Tellingly, the data sets she presented, which spanned different cities across the world, revealed a common pattern of risk and perceptions of risk that disproportionally affect women and girls in their experience and occupation of city spaces. She acknowledged that similar (and in some cases greater risks) were evident for transgender and other minority groups.

Kalms is well aware of the power of visualising this data; she is adept at deploying the findings to underscore both how gender affects engagement with the built environment and the role design can play in reinforcing or subverting these statistical trends. Kalms characterises her approach as neither top-down nor bottom-up. Rather, it is middle-out. She discussed how this approach can incentivise government and a range of other stakeholders to step up and instigate change. And in doing so - how design can make tangible the experiences of under-represented communities in urban space.

Pin up!

Alongside these presentations was an exhibition of works curated by *Kerb's* Gary Ward. The exhibition included photography, illustration and video works that responded to the theme of the evening. Works by Maya Borjesson, PJ Calhoun, Zoe Milah DeJesus, Je sika Ellul, Jixuan (Solomon) Guo and Akira Ode-Smith produced a diverse and captivating range of responses to the thematics of this *Kerb* edition, as well as serendipitous links to what was being discussed upstairs.

Wrap up!

The process of writing this piece continued past the final days of the federal election campaign to its immediate aftermath. It was a campaign notable for the disparity of approach across Australia's two major political parties: business-as-usual tactics from one party and a bold agenda for change from the other. Ultimately it was the former that won, resoundingly. Shocked political commentators diagnosed that the surprise win was due to the other party running a campaign with too many big, bold ideas. This analysis should give us pause to consider the agency of design in a climate (pun intended) that sees bold ideas, change and alternative approaches as unpalatable political risks. It should also be our call to action as designers to examine our own agency and advocate for the changes we think are important. Mintern and Robinson, Davidge and Kalms offer three excellent case studies for how to do just that.

Sofija Kaljević

Detail of the Monument on Freedom Hill Ilirska Bistrica, Slovenia 1965.
Image Valentin Jeck,
commissioned by The Museum of Modern Art, 2016.

YUGOSLAVIA

Arnold Hauser[1] wrote that the past is profoundly without a meaning, without a shape; the past gets its value and significance only in relation to the living present. Through time, every new present could re-create a different past in order to contextualise contemporary narratives. While our memories have continually been reshaped and reconstructed throughout our lifetime and through lifetimes of different generations, it is imperative for our histories to be reinterpreted and rewritten continually - histories of man, art, literature, architecture and its architects.

This is particularly relevant for architectural practices that occurred in times governed by political ideologies interpreted as hostile and anti-democratic by Eurocentric (Western) scholars, such as twentieth century Eastern European communism. For decades the record of rich Yugoslavian architectural heritage that remained after the dissolution of the state in 1990s had been rarely considered outside the region for which it was originally conceived. The old bipolar model of 'centre and periphery of cultural production has produced a skewed and deeply problematic outlook onto history'[2], including the history of architecture. Positioned on the border between two Cold War coalitions, Yugoslavia produced the new version of mid-century architectural modernism, all to satisfy specific needs of country's "self-management socialism", often portrayed as a "third way". Yugoslavia deliberately defied the politics of East-West divide, pursuing friendly relations with both sides. Moreover, the state became one of the founding nations of Non-Aligned Movement in 1961 and 'forged economic and political bonds with partner nations across Africa, the Middle East, and Asia, many of them entering a process of decolonization after newly gained independence'.[3] This atmosphere of political and social inclusion and cooperation allowed distinct architectural practices and styles to develop. The new climate of relative ideological openness allowed the architects to seek inspiration in the East and West equally and to apply 'notions of modernism to specific local conditions'.[4]

Postwar-socialist Yugoslavia was organised as a federation of distinct nations brought together by the ideology of "brotherhood and unity", and this diversity significantly directed the production of architecture.[5] It was essential for an architect to mediate between the needs of (1) national and ethnic groups of the individual republics, with a focus on their capital cities as agents of local political powers and cultures; and (2) the country's political ideological agenda established from the top down. As such, architecture played a crucial role in the transformation of an unevenly developed and predominately rural country - severely devastated during World War II with some of the highest casualty rates in Europe - into an industrialised and urbanised one. The Majority of domestic architects were schooled outside of the region, and when they returned, they often located their practices in the biggest and most prosperous cities. In order to facilitate the intended rapid modernisation, the state frequently moved skilled designing professionals, from more to less developed parts of the country, to accelerate the progress. At the same time, the state aimed to educate local people through founding new institutions of higher education in the less developed regions.[6]

While multiple architectural typologies were developed to correspond with the specific contextual conditions of the state, all of them were created to essentially encourage socialisation, interaction and progress, as well as to remove any type of biases or segregation, regardless of their primary function (housing, education, public space, tourist facility, or memorial complex). In the 1950s, due to massive migrations from the countryside to cities, the "social housing culture" became the central issue, not only in architectural circles but also in ideological debates. 'Intended to be available to all', Mrduljaš argues, 'functional apartments with modern amenities became a herald for the newly emancipated citizen, especially women who were to be freed from household chores in order to be more broadly included in the workforce and public life'.[7] In collaboration with architects and a broad range of social organisations, exhibitions and symposia were regularly organised by the state to discuss 'economic, technological, and aesthetic aspects relevant to housing and stressed the functional role of the apartment within the work process'.[8] The official publication, an outcome of the First Yugoslav Symposium on Housing Construction in the Cities, stated: 'Special attention must be devoted to the psycho-hygienic conditions of the housing: a rest-period for the recreation and restitution of the working capacity of laborers'.[9] This modern apartment, subsidised by the state and distributed throughout communities based on the size and needs of a family unit, became the symbol of socialist self-management urbanisation.

The other concept developed by designing professionals of this era was a "housing community", new neighbourhoods equipped with all necessary amenities: kindergartens, schools, health centers, retail shops, and community centers.[10] While initially financed by self-management funds, the aim of these communities was to sustain themselves through the active participation of its members in decision-making and governing.[11] Housing communities were often located around, or in close proximity to, "self-managed cultural centres", new cultural landscapes where professional culture, cultural amateurism, entertainment, education and political activism all intervened.[12] These innovative forms of public space usually included an open public area of varied size surrounded by cultural institutions like museums, national theaters, cinemas, galleries, etc.,[13] designed to challenge 'the division between high and popular culture and, at least in theory, between politics and the everyday, making them hubs of socialist modernity and a means of social integration'.[14]

The highest levels of government were actively involved in the so-called "schooling explosion", which influenced illiteracy rates to rapidly decrease after World War II. However, politicians and educators were not the only professionals ambitious about the reform. Architects found these educational institutions to be excellent testing grounds for new pedagogical concepts through experimental social design. Mrduljaš writes: 'A series of interdisciplinary symposia called for the abolishment of traditional teaching formats and rigid typological conventions, stressing instead psychological experience of space and demanding more open configurations'.[15]

Even the commercial facilities - such as luxurious tourist resorts on the Adriatic Sea visited by international celebrities, politicians, and gamblers - were designed to facilitate openness and the integration of the local community. Ordinary tourists and local inhabitants had free access to expensive facilities and beaches, contradictory to the current highly segregated form of luxury tourism. Kulić writes: 'Ultimately, most commercial tourism facilities themselves came to effectively function as social condensers: from the coast to the mountains, from the lakeside towns to inland spas, hotels with their restaurants, bars, and open-air terraces almost invariably served not only the visitors from elsewhere, but also local communities as their social hubs'.[16] Permeable lobbies, restaurants, and terraces invited unrestricted access and aimed to connect guests not only with nature but with local community as well.

To execute huge infrastructure projects in a war-ravaged country already lacking an educated work force and technology, "mass volunteer labor" was a matter of practical necessity. "Youth labour campaigns", on the one hand provided a much-needed work force, and on the other created opportunity for upward social mobility through various kinds of trainings in the construction sites, from basic literacy to professional skills. Kulić explains: 'There was a great deal of genuine enthusiasm in this early period, as millions of new brigadiers built new roads, railway lines, dams, irrigation canals, factories, and cities'.[17] Many willingly participated in these projects, regardless of wealth, status, gender, and education, paid only with food, water, and shelter. The vivid memories of these collective events are still very much alive and readily narrated by the oldest members of ex-Yugoslavian societies.

Only when the narratives of Yugoslavian architecture are juxtaposed with the story of contemporary practices of the same group of professionals, does it become clear how, essentially, the goals and objectives of all design professions changed in less than forty years. The work of Lefebvre[18], Harvey[19] and other key scholars from the fields of urban sociology, geography and economics explains that the process of urbanisation, establishment and development of cities and city life, was and still is central to the accumulation of assets and the smooth running of the capitalist agenda. Shoshana Zuboff pushes the idea further by claiming that the city, a shared public space built for human engagement, became a petri dish for the 'reality business of surveillance capitalism';[20] the phase of capitalism where the accumulation of wealth equals the amassment of human behavioural data by particular tech giants. Companies like Google (Alphabet), Cisco, Uber and many others, introduced and legitimised the concept of 'for-profit city'[21] through the model of smart cities, while the implementation of Internet of Things, real-time data processing, cloud computing, etc. - within the public realm - is part of the inevitable future of our cities. Suffice to say that our movements in public space, our intentions, interactions, communication, socialisation, our realm of freedom[22] should not ever be ruled and controlled by these technological advances.

So, what is the role of our profession(s) in this future and why we are questioning it so loudly now? Throughout the history of mankind, architects usually "served the wealth" - maecenas, patrons, kings, aristocrats, churches, industrialists - and today we "serve the extreme wealth": real-estate lords and tech entrepreneurs. In his insightful analysis of repeatedly failed and pointless architecture, Joshua McWhirter argues that the discipline has made a regular habit 'of absolving itself of complicity in the questionable ethics'[23] of built environment development. Through the critique of the new, economically segregated neighbourhood of Hudson Yards in New York, McWhirter claims: 'Architecture is notoriously insular and in denial of its own potentially destructive power over the process of shaping the social fabric of cities'. He asks, 'Can we ask architects why they can't just say no? Or why they won't?'. In attempting to improve our urban living conditions, David Harvey[24] argues how scholars and professionals mistakenly attempt to answer the question: 'What kind of cities do we want to build?'. Instead, he claims, we should ask ourselves first: 'What kind of people do we want to be?'

Whenever Western scholars discuss Yugoslavia, the word "utopia" inevitably turns up. In Western scholarship, Yugoslavia was a utopian political apparatus that produced utopian life, had utopian ideas for the future of man, and consequently it produced utopian architecture. Therefore what was so utopian about that time? Probably the fact that architects, landscape architects, and urban planners, and other professionals, actually considered communal well-being first; they shaped and implemented the policies rooted in the utopian idea of equality and better life for all; and promoted social responsibility throughout the discipline. Designers were educated and trained not only as professionals, but as social activists as well. The architects' expanded agency enabled new forms of socialisation, in which different modes of life intertwined in public arenas. We examine this historic period of a now non-existent state only by looking through the lens of the political/ economical capitalist framework of the present. And, as such, it is clear why Yugoslavian architecture was (sadly) utopian.

It is deeply tragic that the noble force that motivated generations of designers represents a thing of utopia today, and moreover, it is characterised, interpreted, and historically categorised as such. After the sudden, but not unexpected, rise of "social-democratic" movements in the United States in past few years - mostly through Presidential candidacy of Bernie Sanders in 2016 - the resulting new political atmosphere opened the door for an exhibition at the Museum of Modern Art (MOMA).[25] Consequently, it created conditions for the history of Yugoslavian architectural practice to be rewritten and reinterpreted, and for the memory of its achievements to be recovered, hopefully to contribute to the architectural practices of our contested present.

Valentin Jeck

Toward a Concrete Uptopia: Architecture in Yugoslavia, 1948–1980

For the exhibition 'Toward a Concrete Utopia', which was on view at the Museum of Modern Art in New York until January, the Swiss photographer Valentin Jeck went on a journey through time in the former Yugoslavian countries. He photographed architecture from the period of 1948 to 1980. He first visited Macedonia, followed by Serbia, Montenegro, Croatia, Slovenia, Serbia, Bosnia and Herzegovina, and Kosovo.

These photographs are now part of the permanent collection of the Museum of Modern Art in New York.

After World War II, imposing buildings were erected in Yugoslavia, which symbolised the modern attitude to life. Many of them are public buildings. Special and unique are the monuments that commemorate the resistance against fascism in the countries of former Yugoslavia. They are a mixture of sculpture and architecture.

The Battle of Sutjeska Memorial Monument Complex
in the Valley of Heroes Tjentište,
Bosnia & Hercegovina 1971

Flower Monument Jasenovac,
Croatia 1966

Ilinden Memorial Kruševo,
Macedonia 1974

Kolašin Municipal Assembly Kolašin,
Montenegro 1975

Monument to the Uprising of the People of Kordun and Banija Petrova Gora National Park, Croatia 1981

Monument to the Fallen Soldiers of the Kosmaj
Detachment Kosmaj Mountain Park,
Serbia 1971

Monument to the Revolution of the
People of Moslavina Podgarić,
Croatia 1967

Monument on Freedom Hill Ilirska Bistrica, Slovenia 1965

Shrine to the Revolution' or 'Monument to Fallen Miners On Partisan Hill in Mitrovica, Kosovo 1973

Hong Kong's Special Administrative Region (SAR) status, and its unique manifestation as a modern city, is no accident. Its unique identity and laws have been borne out of a combination of the history of British and Chinese ownership, its relationship with contemporary China and, more notably, its long history of protest. As the island was returned to Chinese control in 1997, Hong Kong's unique arrangement with the Chinese Communist Party was a result of its population's willingness to stand up for its beliefs. As Chinese control has begun to encroach on the territory, important protests have occurred in response. These protests, significantly the Umbrella Movement, have offered a new way to think of space and its production, on an island so lacking in places to gather.

Hong Kong has less public space than almost any city in the world, only about one-and-a-half metres per resident.[1] Most of this is public roads, though ninety-nine per cent of citizens rely on the Mass Transit Railway (MTR) - arguably the best mass transit in the world - that requires another large portion of public space. The MTR regulates that they can squeeze in up to four passengers per square metre.[2] Of the remaining public space, most is vertically stacked and privately owned. Miles of foot bridges, outdoor escalators and expansive patios connect roads and transit infrastructure with hundreds of shopping malls and corporate campuses. They blur the edges of public and private space, just as their government blurs the lines of public and private leadership. Property is all on extended lease from the state, with values that have surged 242 per cent in the past decade.[3] The skyline has become a "who's who" of architects, competing on behalf of global corporations for the tallest spire and most lustrous facade. Since establishment as a SAR of China, Hong Kong Island has become the magnum opus for capitalists shaking loose 155 years of colonial stricture.

However, the global mechanism that Hong Kong represents competes with a far longer lived tradition of Hongkongers as dissenters. Famously pragmatic protesters, their demands often opened dialogue with Great Britain. Protests had yielded them the precedent of direct election of eighteen public officials.[4] Political autonomy became ingrained in Hongkongers' identity. Even during Beijing's Tiananmen Square protests in 1989, eighteen per cent of all Hongkongers gathered at the Chinese embassy to demonstrate solidarity.[5] In anticipation of the government handover on 1 July 1997, the date became an annual holiday to celebrate this identity and exercise their freedom of speech. China had claimed it would honour a 'one country, two systems' approach to governing Hong Kong democratically, but anti-subversion laws and restrictions to direct election spurred large protests in 2002, 2007 and 2012. In 2014, restrictions were announced to the nomination of the Chief Executive, and these again met with protests. The student group, Occupy Central with Love and Peace, gathered in Tamar Park, beneath the overarching Central Government Complex in Admiralty. The longer the protesters were ignored, the more their numbers grew. The state found creative ways to repeatedly push them out of the public green spaces, even staging a pro-China counter-protest. The students were pushed to the edges: footbridges, sidewalks and alleys. When police erected temporary

The encampment in Admiralty, 2014.
Photo credit: Wing1990hk

Harcourt Road in Admiralty, 2014.
Photo credit: Pasu Au Yeung

Protesters using umbrellas as shields from the police and later, tear gas, 2014.
Photo credit: FX Pasquier

Umbrella Movement leader giving a speech while using the footbridges of Admiralty as a mezzanine, 2014.
Photo credit: FX Pasquier

fences, the students used zip ties to reconfigure them as protection. When permanent fences locked them out, the students covered them in yellow ribbons, to represent democracy.[6] Every strategy employed by the state to move or remove them was met by increased numbers and conviction within the occupied spaces. On 22 September 2014, students began to move into the only public space in Admiralty larger than Tamar Park: Harcourt Road. They used the nine-lane highway as foundation for the landscape of their democratic vision. Their transient tent community proved to be the most important urban landscape in China later that night, when police flooded it with eighty-seven canisters of tear gas.[7] Protesters refused to abandon the space, using umbrellas as shields from the fumes and taking turns leaving the area to wash their eyes.[8] Meanwhile, two new occupations shut down primary vehicular arteries in Causeway Bay and Mong Kok. This became known as the Umbrella Movement, a symbol of the common man now used as a shield from oppression. Like water between rocks, protesters found space between the monuments of capitalism to counter-produce space that provided for their needs: shelter, food, education, art and community. They created personal private spaces and communal public spaces to serve as libraries, classrooms and gardens.[9] Tens of thousands of protesters fortified their tents with wood, duct tape and zip ties and settled in for what would become an eleven-week occupation.

Spatial power was revealed by the tactics of common people working directly upon the city's architecture. The encampments vacated sidewalks and footbridges, encouraging pedestrians to travel around, above and through them. Public balconies became amphitheatres for Movement leaders. Layered footpaths became galleries for Umbrella Art. The expansive windows of neighbouring shopping malls became a showcase for the working class and students to demonstrate their vision of Hong Kong as greater than an economic engine. From the upper floors of the world's most luxurious malls, shoppers watched the protesters cook their food, tend their gardens and create art. These mundane demonstrations of humanity questioned the value of the systems otherwise occupying the space.

Henri Lefebvre, in pondering the 'right to the city' in the 1960s, insisted that only the daily practices within the city could create the vision for it. He described this process of extrapolating the day-to-day as transduction.[10] Activity similar to that of the occupation could already be found in working class neighbourhoods with the most limited public space. In Mong Kok, each residents' approximate two-thirds of a square metre of public space might be an alleyway or staircase, repurposed as a gathering space for meals or a smoke when required.[11] The Umbrella Movement tested the bounds of transduction by bringing these tactics to Hong Kong Island's most sterile environments in Admiralty and Causeway Bay. These same behaviours became subversive in this new territory, directly challenging the functional intentions of the architecture and the systems that made it possible.

Democracy is inherently iconoclastic; its monument is empty space.[12] Wherever this negative space exists, it can be mobilised to counter the reproduction of capital. It is only these local notions, born from the spaces in between, that can challenge the institutions around them. The Umbrella Movement broke beyond the narrow perceptions of the city's inhumane design to assert that it is only humanity that makes a city; and only humanity that can decide its future.

Emily Schlickman

NEW EYES ON THE STREET

EXPERIMENTING WITH THE ROLE OF SURVEILLANCE TECHNOLOGY IN EVALUATING THE SOCIAL PERFORMANCE OF SMALL URBAN SPACES

We live in an era where cameras are on nearly every street corner. Issues regarding privacy and inequity are, understandably, on many people's minds. What type of data is being collected? How long is information being retained for and by whom? And is this process evenly distributed across all urban populations?

This visual essay explores the topic of surveillance by unpacking a recent research project by SWA's XL Lab entitled 'Plaza Life Revisited'. The project reconsidered the work of William H Whyte to understand how urban spaces, and the people using them, have changed 40 years after the publication of *The Social Life of Small Urban Spaces*.[1] For the project the research team analysed small urban spaces in New York City using many of Whyte's original data collection tools while also experimenting with, and critically evaluating, the surveillance-related technology of machine learning. Based on the idea that people vote with their feet, the research effort sought to anonymously capture anyone and everyone who passed through these small urban spaces - from the pantsuited attorney to the stroller-pushing nanny. The project fundamentally questioned the role of surveillance in identifying overlooked social patterns to aid designers in creating more vibrant public space.

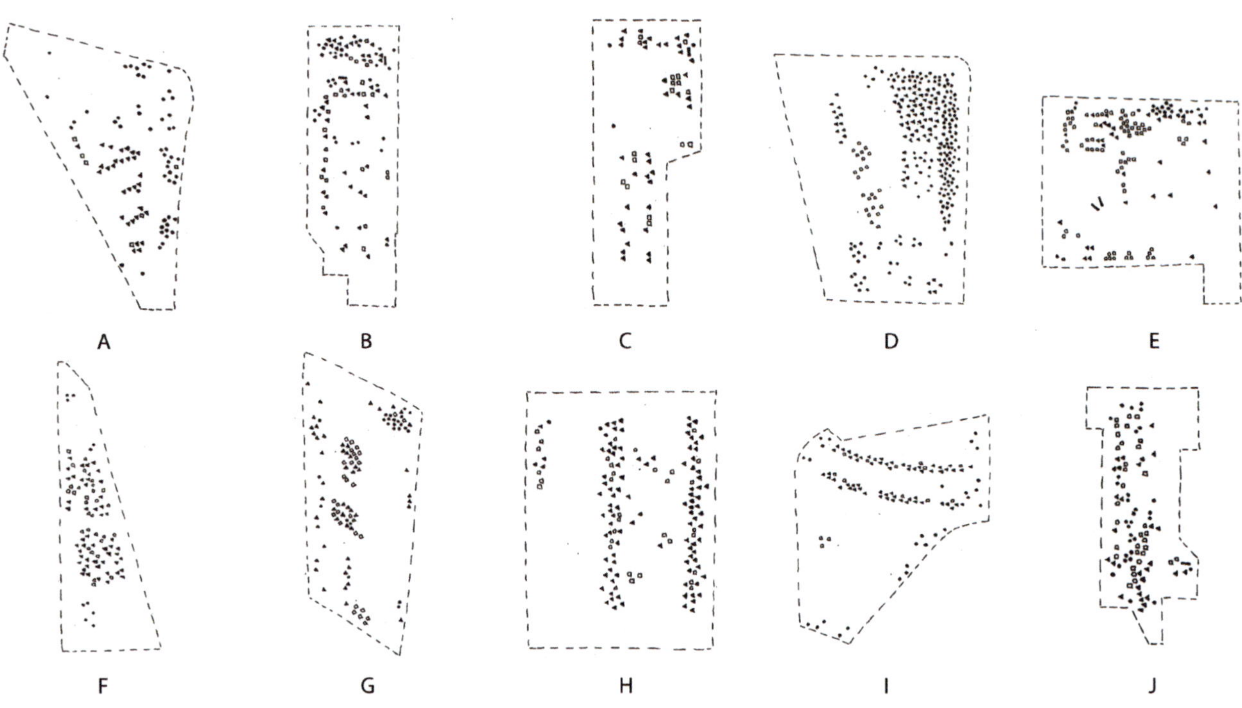

The team used many of Whyte's original data collection tools, including direct observation and hand tabulation, to map pedestrian activity. Here, the research team mapped pedestrian activity during lunch hour.

LOW TRAFFIC HIGH TRAFFIC

One observational take-away from the study was called "Chit-chat Mooring". When small groups of people were observed congregating around an object, even if they were not using it.

One output of the machine learning process was a heat map showing low-traffic areas in light blue to high-traffic areas in green. It provided a snapshot of the social life in each of the urban spaces.

To create the heat maps, the team captured video footage which was run through a machine learning algorithm to understand the spatial distribution of people within each site. Here, the algorithm is identifing, counting, and tracing pedestrian movement.

Claire Martin

POPS AS PROTAGONIST

LANDSCAPE ORDINANCE: THE NEW PUBLIC SPACE MANDATE

Urbanisation and neo-liberal globalisation have brought privately owned public spaces (POPS) to the fore as spectacularised products of, rather than antidotes to, the city. In the context of burgeoning urban populations, reductions in access to public space, ecological threats and dwindling municipal budgets, how can we move beyond the binary of public and private space?

The historical western context for the privatisation of public space dates to landlordism and the enclosure movement of seventeenth- and eighteenth-century England,[1] which continued into the next century with the creation of London's fenced garden squares. By the mid-twentieth century POPS were most commonly understood as urban forecourts, commercial plazas, through-site links and open spaces. Spaces like the Seagram Building Plaza, studied by William H Whyte in the 1979 documentary *The Social Life of Small Urban Spaces*, began to emerge as developers traded floor area for generous zoning concessions and uplifts. By the 1990s, the twin phenomena of deregulation and urbanisation had led to a reduction in the number of public buildings and an escalation of the large-scale corporate ownership of previously publicly accessible spaces.

Public space and private interest

The *2013 Charter of Public Space* definition of public spaces as 'places publicly owned or of public use, accessible and enjoyable by all for free and without a profit motive…' is central to the critique of POPS. Their public value is often seen to be diminished when owners and operators regulate access, use and behaviour (including photography, interviews, protests, sleeping and drinking); restrict access by closing off areas for private development or periodic events; or prevent access entirely through a concentration of wealth and investment that locates POPS in more affluent parts of cities. This has led to many cities mapping the location of POPS and mandating signage to help the public recognise space that is legally required to be accessible to them. Equally POPS may fail to enable the community to recognise itself[2] through conspicuous theming, a lack of local identity or by branding with naming rights. As the number of POPS grows, it seems there is a tension between the accelerated production of our cities and the time it takes for designers, legislators and the community to make truly democratic space.

In the North American context of philanthropy, private donations previously earmarked for education and cultural institutions have begun to flow to open space. In 2012, John Poulson made a single donation of US$100,000,000 to New York's Central Park. Similarly, donations to the High Line have now exceeded over US$150,000,000. But, like bequests to cultural institutions before them, they tend to benefit parks that can generate the most revenue. The much-lauded High Line has both captured the public imagination and created unrealistic expectation – attracting three million visitors a year, but at an annual operational cost of US$3,000,000.[3] Similarly, the iconic Millennium Park in Chicago cost US$500,000,000 to develop and US$6,000,000 a year to operate.[4] Both parks rely almost entirely on private or self-funding for their ongoing operation.

The public value equation

In 1995, Mark Moore from Harvard's Kennedy School posited that public value refers to the 'value created by government through services, laws, regulation and other actions'. His study established numerous ways to define the dimensions of public value including social and cultural value, political value (democratic dialogue and public participation), ecological value and social value, and the protection of citizens' rights. But Moore also argued that it is not who *produces* public value that makes it, instead, it is a matter of who *consumes* it, distinguishing that 'private value [is] consumed individually … whereas public value is consumed collectively'[5].

Ownership and uncertainty – a context for change

It is the coalescence of the private ownership of large swathes of our cities and the existential threat of climate change that demands the reconceptualisation of the role of POPS and the unlocking of their true public value. Ecological systems don't discern between the binary oppositions of public and private, and no single government agency, private corporation or professional discipline can deal with this complexity. We can't design our way out of massive uncertainty but we can advocate, innovate and legislate to put the environment, and not just people, at the centre of place making. In the context of cognitive dissonance, we need to engage citizens in the fundamental decisions that are being made about our public realm, and in difficult conversations about the future of our cities.

New modes of governance

Public space is an integral part of our networked cities whether for recreation, movement, habitat or a sense of place. It is through a desire to see more meaningful, site-specific development contributions that new modes of governance have emerged.

Collaborative planning better acknowledges the importance of involving multiple stakeholders. Innes and Booher, collaborative planning theorists, suggest that some people see 'the increasing hegemony of neoliberalism ... less in terms of de-regulating and privatizing the public realm, but rather as dismantling old divisions between state and market to accommodate new synergistic partnerships'[6]. Governance structures are shifting, with the formation of such entities as the Greater London Authority (GLA) and the Greater Sydney Commission (GSC) that promote the integration of different levels of government decision-making.[7]

The evolution of planning mechanisms, whether codified or discretionary, incentivised or mandatory, has necessitated rigorous needs assessments that have the potential to diversify public space typologies and improve both qualitative and quantitative landscape performance and character. Examples include Seattle's Green Factor, China's Sponge City and the London Plan. In January 2019, the Mayor of London, Sadiq Khan, confirmed that work had begun on the Public London Charter, which will be published alongside the new London Plan, setting 'out the rights and responsibilities for the users, owners and managers of public spaces irrespective of land ownership'. Emphasising that POPS 'should be open, free to use and offer the highest level of public access ... [and only have] rules restricting the behaviour of the public that are considered essential for safe management of the space'[8].

There has been a gradual shift to Integrated Development – or more systems-based approaches – which is the delivery of strategic and local infrastructure, ensured by public, private, community and voluntary sectors planning and working together. In the United States, Community Development Corporations (CDCs) are non-profit, community-based organisations focused on revitalising local areas that, as Gustav Spohn explains, 'function somewhat like private developers but are governed by the community ... [their] boards of directors are typically composed of community residents together with experts who advise them on the technical aspects of fund-raising and development projects. They depend heavily on [both] government and private philanthropic funds, which in turn leverage financing from banks and other investors, their goal is not to turn a profit but to generate economic renewal'[9].

The American city of Seattle heralded several, now superseded, Community Owned Public Space strategies that serve as enduring benchmarks, including neighbourhood matching funds and parks levies. Neighbourhood matching funds occur all around the world and support neighbourhood-based groups that 'want to make creative improvements to local public land ... actively involving the community and building neighbourhood connections'[10]. Community groups are provided with funds based on demonstrated, equivalent contributions from volunteer labour, in-kind donations and other funding sources[11] and are scalable as a model. The park levy initiative was used to fund the acquisition, development, environmental stewardship, maintenance and programming of parks, and required regular voter approval as well as oversight of how the parks were being managed.

We need to engage with procurement and governance of public space in a context of uncertainty by placing more emphasis on the instrumentality of landscape to enable citizens to democratically engage – to truly convey what they value. By understanding how inextricable and interdependent the social, cultural, ecological and economic measures of public value are, we can re-conceive of twenty-first century privately owned public spaces as landscape ordinance. Landscape as a new public institution not defined by the ideologies of neo-liberalism, colonialism and professionalism that maintain existing power relations, but instead mandated by the public through rite and ritual.

Charlie Clemoes

For designers to realise socially responsible design they need to have a degree of control over what they do. However, much of this control is given away in the typical relationships that they enter into in order to work. Whether it's a freelance arrangement with a client or an employment contract with a company, the designer is rarely able to follow an ethical stance without navigating the whims of someone above them in the food chain.

It's not the designer's fault that they end up in these restrictive relationships; in our current economic system we have to work (sell our labour) in order to live. This puts an enormous pressure on even the most ethical designers to sacrifice some (or all) of their scruples in order to sustain themselves and their practice. After all, there's little money in socially responsible design. The kinds of people that need it can't pay for it, and gone are the days of government underwriting the ideal that 'nothing is too good for the working classes'.[1] There's lots of money, meanwhile, in branding for a big multinational, devising the urban plan for a gated community or architecting for a company that builds prisons or border fences.

Out of this depressing state of affairs has come a widespread tendency for designers to earn a living in some unrelated industry or only sell-out part time, in order to spend the rest of it doing what they actually care about. But beyond a partial withdrawal from the mainstream industry, there's another thing a designer can do to exercise power over their work: they can organise in their workplace or collectivise.

There's an obvious reason why this idea has never really caught on in the design professions (at least in the Global North). Unions are traditionally seen as the refuge of exploited unskilled workers. Many designers would instead consider themselves skilled workers doing what they love, and certainly not in need of the kind of collective protections that unions offer (despite the increasingly precarious situation many designers now find themselves in). But leaving aside the basic economic benefits afforded by a union, this kind of collectivism also offers the kind of counterpower which can keep a company in check, ensuring they remain socially responsible.

This may seem overly idealistic, but there are some very instructive examples of how this kind of workplace activism can play out in reality. Take the International Longshore and Warehouse Union (ILWU), a trade union, which represents dock workers on the West Coast of the United States,

Hawaii, and British Columbia in Canada. Established in 1937, the ILWU is considered among the "aristocracy of the working class" in the US because of its ability to ensure its members have excellent salary and benefits. Yet, in spite of their privileged position, members of the ILWU have pursued a number of high-profile boycotts over the years since the union's establishment. In the late 1930s, the ILWU refused to load weapons for fascist countries, at a time when Western governments were all too happy to appease these countries' increasingly aggressive foreign adventures. In the post-war period, the union supported the resistance against Chile's Pinochet regime, following its US-backed coup against the democratically elected socialist government of Salvador Allende. More recently, following their union's earlier support for the international boycott of South Africa during apartheid, members of the San Francisco Bay Area's ILWU Local 10 chapter refused to cross a picket protesting the Israeli blockade of the Gaza Strip.[2]

What the rank-and-file members of the ILWU have shown for almost a century is that effective and committed organisation brings benefits to working

Artworks by Chiara Santoro

conditions and also allows workers to exercise power above the heads of employers, who are all too often inclined to ignore ethical considerations in the interests of the bottom line. That said, ILWU members are working in an industry that has held a consistent strategic importance to the American economy and there are few workers more critical to the smooth running of the global economy than longshoremen, situated as they are at key chokepoints[3] in the just-in-time supply chains that ensure the smooth flow of contemporary capitalism. It is therefore fair to argue that this kind of power is unobtainable to workers in most other industries. Besides that, the longshoreman's work is a far cry from the work of a designer or architect.

It's helpful, therefore, to turn to an example closer to home: that of tech workers. Designers have a lot in common with tech workers: they often cross paths in the workplace; employers in both industries have a tendency to articulate their employees not as workers but as individuals engaged in something less heavy, like a hobby or a calling (helped along by a seemingly fun, easy-going workplace filled with table tennis tables and gyms); and, both industries use this work-as-hobby articulation to excuse the extremely exploitative work patterns they force their employees into.

The debate around the tech industry's "crunch culture" - whereby workers are encouraged to push themselves harder than normal in order to meet a particular deadline - has become increasingly hot in recent years, due to particularly egregious examples such as Rockstar's crunch in the lead up to its release of the much anticipated sequel to *Red Dead Redemption*. Here workers averaged weekly hours of fifty-five or sixty (that's six ten-hour days[4]) and the company's CEO casually let slip that it went as high as 100 hours during particularly heavy stretches.[5] In light of such extreme exploitation, it's not surprising that it is here where workers have been ahead of the curve in resisting it.

One of the most radical organisations to emerge from this growing resistance is the Tech Workers Coalition (TWC), founded in 2014 by Matt Schaefer, a software engineer, and Rachel Melendes, a cafeteria worker-turned professional trade union organiser at a tech company. The background of the two founders is instructive of its radical approach to the industry.[6] Challenging this notion of an elite cohort of engineers and designers who are separate from the other (frequently invisible) support staff working in tech, the Tech Workers Coalition points out that the industry requires a huge amount of effective and reproductive labour (such as working in the cafeteria) in order to sustain itself.

The TWC has since been involved in various campaigns supporting the efforts of workers in tech firms to organise, including helping the trade union Unite Here organise cafeteria workers at Facebook.[7] Not stopping there, they have also been very vocal in their opposition to the work that tech companies are engaged in, with their recently-published #TechWontBuildIt zine offering a helpful overview of tech worker protests against their companies' work on projects geared towards general system state violence.[8]

Considering the tech workers' rapid move from workplace grievances to more broad social critique, it's clear that designers would benefit from emulating the tech workers' example, especially if they are to fulfil the initial idealism that likely brought them to the profession in the first place. What both TWC and ILWU clearly demonstrate is that designers can quickly begin addressing the root cause of their powerlessness if they organise collectively.

A SELECTION OF PERCEPTIONS

Public space is experienced by an incredibly diverse range of people. For designers, part of the challenge is to learn, understand and accommodate the public. It is important to remember that these people are not all fellow designers. We design space for people of all ages and genders, and from many places. Each of these people have their own experience: of fear, of comfort, of adoration, of reminiscence. In our desire to increase designers' awareness of the breadth of who our community encompasses, we approached a range of artists to show what being in public feels like to them.

Following is the material that comprised an exhibition we commissioned- to be run as part of our Get Up! event (PG48). Led by one of our editors, Gary Ward, the editorial team curated the formal hanging and subsequent printed publication of this work. We deliberately sought artists of diverse perspectives and practices.

Each responded to our abstract (PG07), and provided a short written statement and visual work.

JIXUAN (SOLOMON) GUO

A Paradise or a Prison?

There is a proverb said, Shenzhen is the paradise, and Sanhe is the prison.

Shenzhen is a major city in Guangdong Province, located in the Special Economic Zone. It's relaxed economic policy has meant Shenzhen's GDP has doubled ten times since 2000. The majority of growth is owing to the assembly and production of products for Apple, Samsung and Huawei. They attract a huge amount of young people from all over China, looking for fortune and a bright future. However, the blue-collar work involves long hours and hard work. The harsh conditions of places like Foxxcon have exhausted the passion and energy of the once exuberant and ambitious young people.

Many have sought a way out by way of the Sanhe job market. The informal economy and odd-jobs earn them around 100 CNY a day, which is enough to live for three days. The higher income opportunity means those in Sanhe work for one day and play for two. However, these jobs are mediated through job agencies. It is common practice for these agencies to take the workers' ID cards, removing their ability to leave (ID cards are required to buy things like train tickets). Pleasure and relief is sought in the virtual world, playing online games and gambling.

After a while, these young men who came to Shenzhen with their dreams gradually lost their direction and hope in Sanhe. Even the workers who are still persevering through the hard work in Shenzhen; they still can't have their own happiness. They don't have local resident identification status in Shenzhen, so they can't buy vehicles, apartments or have their children educated. The door to freedom for the young people will always be open, however, the road for them is always blocked.

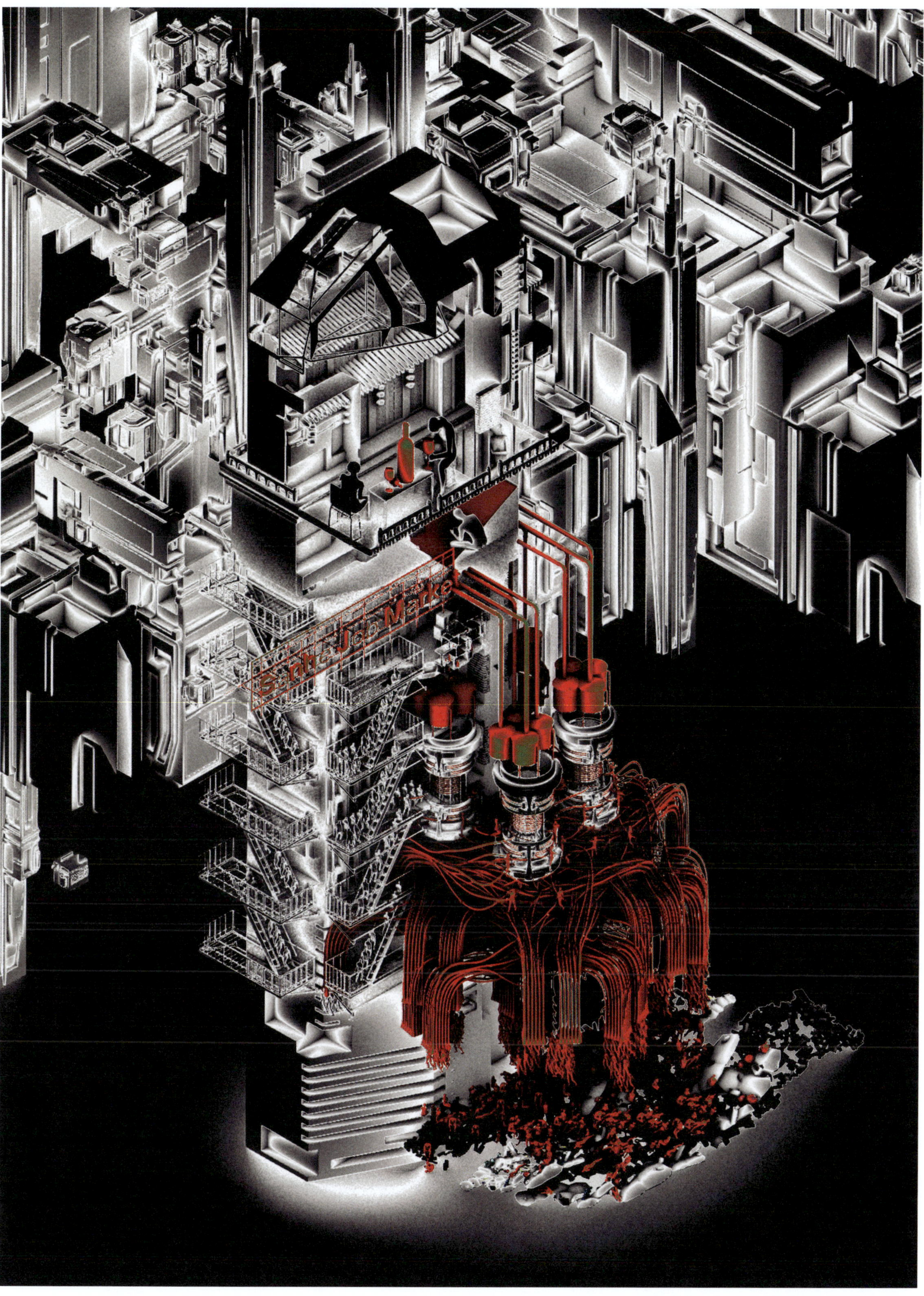

AKIRA ODE-SMITH
Pastime Paradise

In responding to the *Kerb* 27 brief, *Pastime Paradise* draws from the critical text *Blueprint for Counter Education*. Following its diagrammatic process and modernistic graphical fashion; a style associated with the Sex Pistols to *Ray Gun* magazine. What you see are raw manifestations of thought that deal with the paradigms of exclusivity, leading the reader/viewer to wonder and question how to approach the issues outlined in *Kerb* 27. In this piece I also question an Australian Identity and the associative overly masculine domain. I look to use this artwork and the concerns *Kerb* holds, as a springboard to reflect on our current paralysis as a society.

HERO OF THE "DISCOVERED TERRITORY"
THE AUSTRALIAN TYPE"
A FAIR GO
EGALITARIAN
ANTI-AUTHORITARIAN
ASSLESSNESS
MULTICULTURAL
BURBAN
MEDIOCRACY
WAY OF LIFE
FREE
COMMONWEALTH
latrobe
influencing
cultural
content
within
pre deliniated
limits
What if we replaced the daily newspapers with the likes of
THE LIFTED BROW
GUSHER mAGAZINE
THE new Philosopher
Womankind
NO CURE
Peppermint
The MONTHLY
SwampLand
Monster
Children
Dumbo
Feather
we must learn how to craft stories
and they became what they beheld
SUBVERSIVELY
CHOSEN ART & LITERATURE
MASCULINE DOMAIN
EXPLOITATION
TAME
THE LANDSCAPE
COLONISE
LEGITIMISING
CODING NATIONALISTIC SENTIMENT
1901
If the problem was at this scale: what would you do?
1:1 1:5 1:10 1:20
1:50 1:100 1:200
1:500 1:1000
have a pen? circle where you feel comfortable

CAROLINA CATROLA

Creating this piece, for me, was about getting in touch with my senses. As an artist, I believe that I'm sensitive to everything that surrounds me, which sometimes can be overwhelming. Making an illustration about neurodivergent or autistic people in sensorial cities made me wonder about how would it be if the surrounding spaces took all of my energy, or hurt me by being too intense. I had to put myself in other peoples shoes and look at the urban space, paying attention to each sound, each colour, each dynamic. One does not do that on a regular bases. It opened my perception, it was a sort of awakening. Being aware of every single thing just by walking my daily route from work to home was exhausting! I'm usually on my thoughs, listening to my music or reading a book. Suddenly I became nervous and anxious. So, in order to portray that, I created an illustration of two little boys (and they look the same on purpose, it's kind of the same coin but two sides of it), in a regular street, but the one on the left sees everything "normal", and for that I draw the buildings from the right perspective, the colours used are pastels, that are very gentle and smooth colours giving a sense of relaxation.
On the right side, there is the boy that represents neurodiversity. His vision is all distorted and giving a sense of dizziness, the colours used are almost fluorescent, crashing into one's eyes. And the sound is represented by the red waves, almost like a net, that is coming to catch us.

Artitive app

-

Hold your smartphone in front of the artwork

-

calhoun.com.au

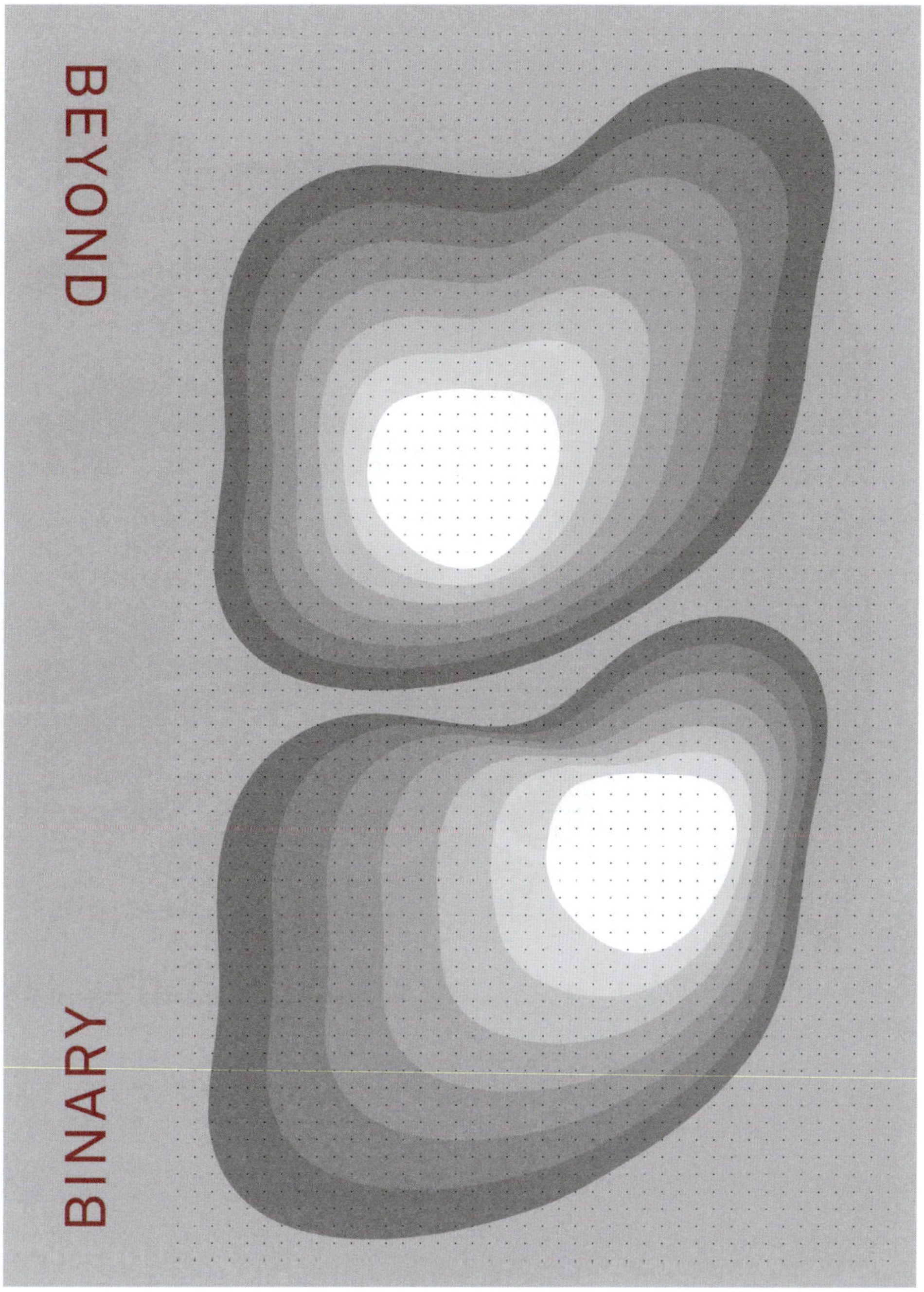

PJ CALHOUN

Beyond Binary

Gender identity and the physical body are sometimes intertwined but have separate design considerations. The needs of non-binary, transgender, intersex, and otherwise gender diverse people are not being met though binary design. We should perhaps consider design in terms of designing for a physical need (body), and or an identity need (inclusivity).

There is hope of a new generation of designers and developers who are more focused on community building than place making. The artist recently observed a well executed, sustainability and community focussed design development by Wolff projects, in Roseneath Street, Clifton Hill. They feel the next step with similar urban projects is to invest more research into the broader range of identities of the users in our urban communities.

As a graphic designer, and from their perspective as a non-binary identifying person, they want to show the distinction between gender identity and the physical body. They have done this by using the visual language of *Kerb Journal's* core audience to express these concepts visually.

ZOE MILAH DEJESUS

Woman's World

The city in this scene encourages women to live their life without fear. In terms of gender, women experience parks/public space in a very different way to men. My response to the *Kerb* abstract was to draw focus on women using space in a way men are permitted to do. I want to highlight everyday activities to call out just how precarious women's freedom in public space is, especially their freedom to be and to be safe.

MAYA BORJESSON
Abraxa

'...corporate buy-in has created an increasingly homogenous built environment.' (Editorial, PG07.)

Assuming 'corporate buy-in' refers to the existence of developers, the way in which planning and development currently operates in Melbourne means that it is almost essential for developers to be involved. Without developers who would fund/build developments? Multi-residential developments create affordable housing options for both renters and buyers. There is an efficiency in design and cost with stacking floorplates and repeated details, a tried-and-true logic that drives multi-residential design. If every new multi-residential development was bespoke, we could be at risk of creating a streetscape of mis-matched competing architecture that would certainly come at a cost premium. The question is whether efficiency can be elegant? For the majority of build contracts, the original designer is novated to the developer, so it is not just the designer but also the developer that is responsible for the aesthetics of our streetscape. This series of photos looks to challenge the perception that multi-residential developments are inferior and highlight the elegance in the rhythm and repetition of a 'homogenous built environment'.

Magdalena Sliwinska

SENSITIVE BELONGING IN A PUBLIC SPACE

Our physical and emotional bodies carry traumas and nervous tensions that look like distorted, sagging and ungrounded bodies, unable to connect to others with presence. This equally can be seen reflected in the abandoned, distorted elements of the city. The anxious mind is, to me, a tethered product of commercial growth. But with the proposition of a city built for hyper-speed economic generation and exponential mental illness - that some say is its by-product - what is the individual's experience of the city, and how does design and the act of designing sit within it?

There is growing awareness of the increasing rate of anxiety in our society, which also affects students of architecture.[1] A 2014 study by Parlour 'Guides to Equitable Practice' has identified that 'depression, anxiety and low self-esteem ... can flow into other areas of work - for example, poor decision-making, difficulties identifying priorities and weak negotiating skills'.[2] A question needs to be asked: how can anxious and depressed young designers plan spaces for the benefit of citizens when they themselves are not coping and managing their mental health?

People with anxiety and depression find themselves more vulnerable to social isolation and loneliness[3], including highly sensitive people or empaths who are twenty per cent of the population and feel invisible in a world that doesn't value sensitivity.[4]

If 'architectural and artistic meanings are always existential meanings' that say to us 'this is how it feels to be a human being in this world,'[5] then what does the experience of walking through a frantic and commercial city tell us, both for those with anxiety and those without? In *Architecture of Happiness*, Alain de Botton relates characteristics of a person 'with qualities such as friendliness, kindness, subtlety, strength and intelligence' to those of a building.[6] According to Mirko Zardini, 'fear is a primary force driving the proliferation of socially homogeneous' architecture that 'determines the definition of what is left of public space'[7]. It is time that the increased privatisation of public spaces that controls and constricts our rights and behaviours[8] and contributes to a sense of anxiety re-evaluates its purpose in order to enable human freedoms.[9]

Looking at the recent article 'What is Federation Square for?'[10] a lack of clear cultural values prevails in this civic and communal space in Melbourne. Initially designed as a 'strange attractor' through its 'geometrically intriguing series of shard-like structures and architectural lines'[11], it is now 'withering away' lacking 'spaces to congregate' and clear accessible connection to the natural resource of the Yarra River.[12] The irregular facades are almost impenetrable 'instead of a sensing wall surface that protects and senses' and 'turns the spectator into a participant'[13]. Equally this irregularity highlights the fascination of fragmentation in the modern architectural canon as 'something that represents the society of its time, instead of stability that traditional architecture is supposed to reassure you of'[14].

A public space should reaffirm our commonality, our shared sense of place and our desire to be included.[15] The commonality is our humanness - made up of imperfections, vulnerability and expression - something that an empathic or anxious person seeks through their yearning for spiritual connection.[16] The topic of anxiety or mental health is quite rare and at times absent throughout the pedagogy of the architectural degree[17], but we could rediscover it through cultural expression and understanding of the human psyche.

The lack of a public place connected to its place and culture can create the 'subtle but persistent feeling of being out of place ... lumbering, clumsy, easily distracted'[18]. The missing view of nature and its presence, which 'enhances the feeling of one-ness', can spark a lack of presence that can further lead to the fight or flight response[19] when the body emerges into the 'impersonal dimension of bodily existence'[20]. This impersonality can be further elicited by the lack of engaging personal and private affordances, 'which affects the highly sensitive person with a low threshold for stimulation, the need for alone time ... plus an aversion to large groups'[21].

We need to rediscover the emotional memory of a city through all aspects of the human soul - even those dark memories, as they remind us of a soul.

A city that acknowledges its soul, creates personal experiences for its users. According to Dr Gabor Maté, today's society creates endless separations.[22] Through an understanding of an empathetic or anxious person searching for meaning, we can rediscover our connection to place, history and each other. Our authenticity is necessary for our survival.[23]

If a city is like a sensing body, Krakow in Poland is its ears and sound. The memory of history being whispered – disguised in textures of quiet cries, loud trumpet playing – is emotion inducing. I remember, as I rest with my eyes closed and the window open, the clicking of hooves on a cobblestone, birds singing, the bell sound in a distance, the chatter of voices. It brings me instantly home, through its breathing walls and exhaling sounds.

If sound induces memory, smell and the insight of the nose induces curiosity. Fez in Morocco is a journey of incense smoke, jasmine, frankincense, myrrh and sweet mint tea. This is both enticing and mesmerising and walking through the tight alleys surrounding its historic square, the smells carry you to prayer mosques, twirling Sufis and the high-altitude mountains. This experience requires surrender but, in turn, gifts to you a revelation.

Just like staying close to your heart – a heart that I found in Cusco in Peru and in its square with the Inca king pointing to the mountains. This insight is not taken lightly by the people of Cusco who in the drizzling rain, among the coloured rainbows, sing and dance their traditional songs, reigniting their language – a language of the heart. There are no words to describe and rationalise this experience. All I know is that even in the drizzling rain I feel warmth in my body.

So, as I walk through the streets of Melbourne, I wonder where its heart, ears and nose are, not in the literal sense but as a sensing body. One day, I venture to the undulated landscape of Federation Square filled with infinity, as if our time here never ends. I see the dust of the earth being carried by the wind, scattered onto surfaces. I feel an overwhelming emptiness and stillness, one which makes me feel uncomfortable.

As an extroverted empath, I enjoy spaces that encourage my curiosity but also provide a respite. I was hoping to find that here in this square among the clicking tongues of international communities, seagulls begging for food, the sound from the TV screen showing a tennis match being played. I sensed the competion in this space. I didn't want to play its game, thinking I would never win because of my sensitivity and quietness. I sat on the edge of its middle, which was drenched in the sun yet empty – almost like a washing line full of linen. The only participant in this space was an innocent child, twirling around the space like sheets in the wind. I too joined in, not in the twirling, but in curiosity. I felt the need to walk barefoot on this textured surface, yet the sun burned my soles. I could sense others before me, walking about this land, yet in this moment everyone was too busy watching the screen. The chatter of the voices rose like a wave against the screeching seagulls looking for food. There's energy here but the intimacy is jagged with the overlooking thick facades. The air feels stagnant. My curiosity leaves my body. My job was to come here to write about this space and once I have done so, there is nothing left to do, no sound to bring its stories to warm my heart, no smell to entice me. It is like a mind disconnected from its body.

I often wonder, when I am in the midst of my anxiety, how I can entice myself away from the four walls of my safety. It is often hard to go outside, to pull oneself from the spiralling thoughts and the oncoming pity. I think about what kind of space would feel like an embrace. A space that sees you as you are, makes you present with the surroundings, speaks to your soul and ignites your curiosity. Would its walls be white, or is it a sense that comes from the values and atmosphere of the space? What would a space look like if it made you feel you were enough; that you were loved? Does that space exist? Apart from coming back to yourself, because such interiority can sometimes be suffocating, can we find such a space in the streets and in the public squares? Could we share our vulnerabilities and our humanness at the same time as rejoicing in our communal exchange?

Of all the homes I lived in while growing up, this little Ho my world more than any other. And the one for which I hav in government housing I knew my neighbours. With this the ability to freely explore and learn about the world a later, I have not since experienced the same sense of co people refer to low socio-economic communities with p you feel uncomfortable but for me they bring joy and be

s Westing government unit was the one I believe shaped he fondest memories. Unlike in other homes, while living me a sense of safety and with this sense of safety, came ınd me. More than thirty years and twenty-seven homes munity as I did within this space. It saddens me to hear y. That was not my experience. These photos may make ıtiful memories of the people who inhabit these spaces.

Wendy Scriven

SPACE & CLASS PERSPECTIVE

Lois Nguyen

Beyond All: Re-examining meaning in universal design

Within universal design's mantra of "design for all" is a coded call for erasing disability experiences. Specifically, universal design is consistently promoted as "good design", yet we have not adequately reflected on its application as a potentially harmful design practice. "Good design" and "best design" inconsequentially describe design methods as promoting inclusivity. In this article I will align the three models of how disability is understood to trace how social concepts of disability are expressed. I will suggest an alternative to the current intersection of design and disability by using a cultural model approach. The three primary models used in disability studies to describe how disability is conceptualised are medical, social, and cultural.

The medical model emphasises disability as bodily configuration, requiring treatment, rehabilitation, and cure.[1] Resisting accessible design, or denying its necessity, reflects a medical model of understanding disability. It shifts the responsibility to adjust to the built environment to the user. The error of the inaccessible environment lies in the user's impairment, the solution being to "restore" the individual to the "average" body in order to navigate the inhospitable environment.

The social model emphasises disability as completely external to the body and a result of "disabling" restrictive environments and institutions. While impairment is private, disability is "structural and public".[2] The social model first appeared in the barrier-free design movement. After the mass uptick in citizens with disabilities after World War II, access for veterans coming home to the United States came to the forefront of architecture.[3] Barrier-free design established that removing physical barriers would allow those with disabilities to access public space. Simultaneously, barrier-free design grew with the study of ergonomics.[4] Based on analysis of the body and a normative understanding of wheelchair users, barrier-free design brought the experience of the disabled individual as close to normalcy as possible by removing physical barriers, thus attempting to equalise access to public opportunities. From this evolved the next design and disability relationship: universal design.

The term "universal design" was first used by Ronald Mace, an architect and educator who used a wheelchair his entire life after contracting polio as a child.[5] He was instrumental in passing the first set of accessibility-centred building codes in the United States, and for developing groundbreaking federal legislation.[6] He founded the Center for Universal Design at North Carolina State University. Universal design was initially a design manifesto based on radical epistemic disability activism.[7] Mace blended activism and his desire to mainstream his visions of universal design. He was constantly developing strategies to convince his peers that universal design would not limit their creative capacity and he offered designers 'the chance to challenge conventional design thinking'.[8]

Mace expanded the definition of universal design in 1989 and this responded to the minimum demands of laws which required a few special features for disabled people: it is possible to design most manufactured items and building elements to be usable by a broad range of human beings, including children, elderly people, people with disabilities, and people of different sizes.[9] By the late 1980s, Mace and the Center for Accessible Housing's involvement with the Fair Housing Amendments Act propelled universal design into widespread circulation. And the dilution of universal design as a disability-epistemic activist practice began.

Today universal design has been completely absolved of its original intention to support the value of disability-based knowledge, in the development of variation-based design politics.

Aimi Hamraie highlights popular refrains responsible for making universal design a palatable concept to designers across multiple disciplines: 'accessibility for all is simply good design,' and the suggestion that universal design '...transcends ability with innovation. It's a design that works for everyone'.[10] Its proliferation in the media signified confusing and malleable meaning for the term 'universal design'.

When the Americans with Disabilities Act was passed in 1990, Mace and other disability and design activists lost control over universal design, as a design practice to serve not only those with disabilities, but all 'spatially excluded populations'[11] as universal design came to represent 'broad accessibility'.[12] This shift is made clear in the Center for Accessible Housing's definition in 1991:

> Universal Design means simply designing all products, buildings, and exterior spaces to be usable by all people to the greatest extent possible. It is advanced here as a sensible and economical way to reconcile the artistic integrity of a design with human needs in the environment.[13]

Not only does this definition lose its focus on those with disabilities and the intersection with other spatially excluded populations, it also presents universal design as a "simple" design practice, a "simple" solution. This is contrary to Mace's original call to action in 1985 where he positions universal design as an exciting challenge, the "cutting-edge of progressive design".[14] This point marks the entrance into the post-Americans with Disability Act (ADA) era, setting up universal design to enter its current manifestation as a post-disability narrative. In the post-ADA, neoliberal-market world the once potent language came to 'capitalize on rights discourses, market trends, and new legal landscapes'[15], shifting erratically between activist groups, policy requirements and corporate manufacturers.[16] My troubled observation of universal design as the common catch-all to describe design that is human-centred, accessible for the aging, and, of course, good, boils down to promoting universal design as a useful set of principles that must become "common sense"[17] to every designer.

The retirement of the baby boomer generation created a recent spotlight on universal design, whereby ageing bodies are accommodated by the same legal standards for people with life-long impairments.

While universal design lent a critical layer to the ADA that argued for the need for accessible design to be an aesthetic and meaningful practice, I maintain that with the total omission of "disability" within the principles of universal design it has been reduced to a checklist utilising "all" and "everyone" to be more palatable to able-bodied users. Pre-ADA, universal design sought to discuss oppression, based on disability in the built and usable environment, through design discourse and observe the intersectionality of disability with other qualifiers of marginalisation. However, according to Hamraie, post-ADA era universal design's departure from disability rights discourses operates as if '...civil rights legislation had adequately addressed ableism by creating an equal playing field between disabled and non-disabled people',[18] which follows the social model of disability, albeit in disillusionment. If impairment does not exist because disability exists in the environment, and if the environment has been addressed by the ADA and universal design - and made truly accommodating for "any" and "everybody" - then there must be an "everyone".

As a contrasting viewpoint, I suggest a cultural model approach as the next step in re-acknowledging disability as design knowledge. The cultural model emphasises disability as a subjective state, existing in the interface between the body, embodiment, and the environmental experience. It considers the medicalisation of disability, the fluidity of disability in relation to the contextual environment, and the inseparable bodymind.[19] Contrary to the erasure of disability present in current universal design discourse, the cultural model seeks to acknowledge the stories and experiences that reflect current issues felt in the built environment and recognises that there is not an "everyone" because oppression based on disability persists. In this cultural model approach disability on the individual level means a unique and individual form of embodiment, which "everyone" does not experience. Knowledge extracted from those embodiment-based experiences has the potential to provide infinite perspectives on ways of being in the world and ways of interacting with the landscape. I am more curious about the energy derived from disability ownership, knowledge, and making, which resonated even before the founding of universal design - when disabled activists were creating their own access, taking sledge hammers to the streets in cities across the United States in the 1960s and 70s to create curb cuts.[20] If users and designers, and the blurry mixing between the two, can harness this same energy there are many possibilities for tangible material and intangible social interfaces to occur, as an incubator for disability ownership, knowledge, and making.

Melbourne is Australia's fastest growing urban region. Between 2017 and 2018[1], 119,400 new residents joined the city's cosmopolitan population. To manage the rapid growth[2], the Victorian Government has begun multiple urban renewal projects to increase Melbourne's residential capacity and strengthen its economy. The Docklands precinct, for instance, represents the current trend of corporatised design which gentrifies brownfield sites that, while centrally located, operate outside the city's homogenous structure.

Although this regeneration enhances Melbourne's residential and commercial capabilities, it knowingly excludes the unexpected eco-cultural performances – for example, public sex – and highly modified environmental processes that thrive in the city's most unstructured landscapes. As Kim Dovey[3] explains, Melbourne's renewal 're-codes that which it deterritorialises', and produces 'stable territories and identities' that are strongly influenced by its economic and political systems.

Significantly, the ongoing erasure of peripheral spaces through regenerative design minimises their ability to support diverse cultural expressions, such as cruising, and reinforces biased perceptions of what is considered morally and ecologically suitable for the metropolis.

Using Dovey's ideas of deterritorialisation, re-coding and stability as a guide, the following creative works, titled *THAT'S KAMP*, explore the tensions between extreme renewal, exclusionary design and Melbourne's queer ecosystem through text and photography. The images feature a journey from an unspecified park in central Melbourne to an adjacent marginalised landscape currently in the processes of regeneration. The photos' intent is to foreground and celebrate the aesthetic, spatial and performative qualities of this queer ecosystem before landscape architects and governments substitute it with yet another standardised planting design.

"BEATS EXIST UNE
COMMUN
"YET WHAT'S ADMIRABLE ABOUT BEATS
ORGANISED A WAY OF MEETING THEIR
"VIOLENCE IS RARE, A CO
AND IS WI
"EVEN IN THE WILDERNESS THERE IS DEC
KEEP TO THEMSELVES, DO NO DAMAGE, BO

LY... IMPERILED BY
OUTRAGE”

HOW MEN - GAY, BI AND STRAIGHT - HAVE
EST NEEDS IN... A CIVILISED FASHION”

OF CONDUCT SEEMS TO EXIST,
NGLY OBEYED”

Y, ORDER, EFFICIENCY; THE CRUISERS
R NONE OF THE PARK’S OTHER USERS”[4]

“ARRESTS OF MEN ENGAGED IN OR
SIMILARLY REVEALS NATUR
“AS A PURE SPACE THAT
INCURSIONS OF
“ONE COMMONLY EMPLOYED STRAT
TO EQUATE SEX
“AND TO FOCUS ON THE LITTER
PRODUCED BY

KING FOR SEX IN NATURAL SPACES
PARALLEL CONSTITUTION"
BE PROTECTED FROM THE
C HOMOSEXUALS"
TOWARD THIS EFFECT HAS BEEN
TH POLLUTION"
D DAMAGE TO THE ENVIRONMENT
SEXUAL ACTS"5

"NON-REPRODUCTIVE HOMOSEXUAL SEX
RENDERINGS
"AND ENVIRONMENTALISM AS INCOM
AS HOMOSEXUALITY WAS ASSOCIATE
"THE CREATION OF REMOTE RECREATI
OF HEALTHY GREEN S
"WAS UNDERSTOOD PARTLY AS A T
RAVAGES OF EFFEM

ALSO BEEN REPRESENTED IN DOMINANT
ECOLOGY”[6]
IBLE AND THREATENING TO NATURE
TH THE DEGENERACY OF THE CITY”
WILD SPACES AND THE DEMARCATION
S INSIDE THE CITY“
PEUTIC ANTIDOTE TO THE SOCIAL
E HOMOSEXUALITY”[7]

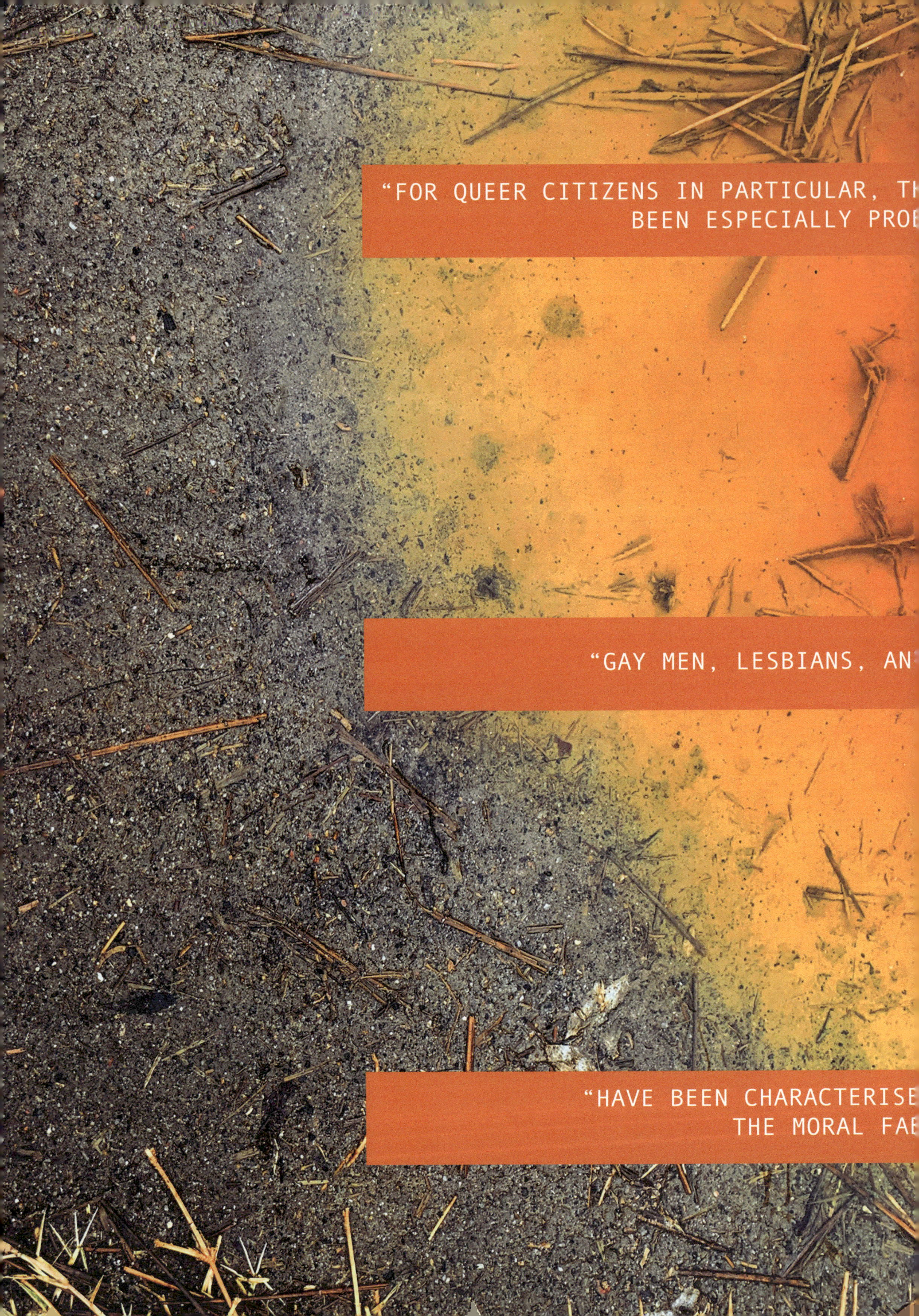
"FOR QUEER CITIZENS IN PARTICULAR, TH
BEEN ESPECIALLY PROB
"GAY MEN, LESBIANS, AN
"HAVE BEEN CHARACTERISE
THE MORAL FAB

LANGUAGE OF ECOLOGICAL PROTECTION HAS
MATIC FOR CENTURIES"
RANSGENDER INDIVIDUALS"
S POLLUTION THREATENING
OF SOCIETY"8

“INNATE CONNECTIONS
“
“AND CONTROLLING DIS

TWEEN PUBLIC SPACE”

”

RSE OF URBAN DESIGN”[9]

Interview with Simone Bliss

Kerb 27 Editorial Team

One of our editors, Shanley Price sat down with Simone Bliss, Founder of SBLA, a Melbourne firm with an approach to work quite different to most. They spoke about the value of different perspectives at work, and how to think differently about the boundary between work and life.

SP: *Kerb 27 has picked up on a tension between, people that have strong ideas about the way work should be, do they try and work within their old existing often larger firm, or do they start their own, with their own set of ideas in mind. Could you speak a little to how you weighed up that tension, when you were thinking of starting SBLA?*

SB: For me, work and life are so directly intertwined that there is no off button. I know of many people who solve their design questions at night, I constantly awake in the middle of the night with a solution to a concept or technical issue that I've been trying to solve. I would argue that our minds aren't made for a nine to five corporate office environment. I was interested in exploring how an office can be tailored to the people that work within it, versus getting projects and then applying staff to resource that project. When I had my daughter I had to make a difficult decision to leave my work family and seek ultimate flexibility. She was (and still is) a terrible sleeper. The thought of sitting at my desk, ready to be my best at 9am – rushing my children out the door to be at child care at 7.30 in the morning didn't appeal to me.

I spoke to many peers about their work places and sought out existing female directors with young children for advice on how to navigate having a child and wanting to continue my career and project types. What happens to you when you do have children or you do have additional interests or needs to landscape architecture and wish to work part time? Why should this be seen as a negative? There is a tension between being a part time employee and an ability to work on large projects that require constant project management. Why can't we job share? Why can't we being with our children for an hour or two during the day be like being in a work meeting? I was feeling disappointed with society's outlook of: if you have a child your priorities change. I don't believe your priorities change, I believe you have an additional priority to add to the mix. With this brings lateral thinking and problem solving, skills that are quite useful to our profession!

If you work part time what do you do, and there were a number of people that came back to me and said 'my role has changed since I asked to be part time', and 'I'm no longer able to work on the type of project or scale of project, therefore I'm given something else, so working on submissions or writing specifications', or doing a sub category of what their previous role was. I was quite interested in starting something to change the profession on a small scale, in thinking about, how this model can offer an alternative.

SP: *So an opportunity to show change*

SB: Yes, and test it. SBLA has had a number of various employee/sub-contractor scenarios over the last three years. It started with collecting talented mothers that were either working for themselves or wanted to get back into the industry. With this offered a much needed support group of like-minded ladies, who were navigating being a new mother and being passionate about their careers. The next scenario was about integrating sole traders with complementary skills to landscape architecture and the next after that was employing more people that wanted to work part time for personal or career related requirements.

SP: *Could you detail some ways that since starting SBLA the work that you do has changed a design perspective?*

SB: Our whole industry works at such a fast pace that not only our lives and health are affected, but so is the design outcome. Short timelines do nothing for good design. We push back on project deadlines where able, I talk to our clients on a personal level and apply a new set of criteria to why a project is undertaken. Projects are weighed up equally on design process/communication merit and design opportunities. Each project is a new relationship, if I feel like the communication or the project isn't going to necessarily fit with our values, then I'm less inclined to take the job. This may not be the best formula for economic success, but I value experience over money.

In terms of the design itself I've been quite interested in the way that schools and educational systems are set up, and how that relates to a work place. So things like if the environment is nurturing, if a school is nurturing, then the ability for children to learn is greater because they feel safe, and they have a framework but they feel like they have an ability to be flexible or adapt within that structure. And I've taken some of those ideas and applied it to the business. So people feel like they have more time, or that time is theirs, therefore the ability to think creatively directly affects their design outcomes. Typical work structures that for some people (myself included) can create an anxiety or pressure, which therefore affects the way by which we design. So my take on it is: if you have a mind that works better at 6am, or a mind that works better at 11pm, work in a way that best suits your individual brain and your way of working. That in turn creates a different way of designing, which promotes more freedom and that affects the design outcome. Interestingly, most people within the office do work typical hours however I believe they feel that flexibility is there should they need it.

SP: *Did you have thoughts about those pressures previous to SBLA? And would you in those instances work or try and push for more flexible working times?*

SB: I sure did and these thoughts were applied. My previous places of work were more inclined to allow a freedom to create and were very people based. My previous directors would employ people based on their personality/ common sense and creative thinking, technical skills followed. These learnings were applied to SBLA.

I read a lot about other practices that allowed people to work based on what suited their individual lives, and there was a lot of information about how people felt freer or more supported and therefore it changed not only the way they did their work, but their role within that office, and the amount that they felt connected to that place. One friend set up a recruitment office where everyone was the director for a month, this approach empowers people and creates equality – I have no doubt this outlook filters into our design outcomes.

We have an office environment where, as long as the projects are planned ahead of time, people are invited to take more than four weeks annual leave. If I'm going to take more weeks off in a year when my children are at school and I need to take school holidays off, why can't other staff do the same? Time away from the office brings inspiration, fresh eyes and rest, this naturally filters into the design outcomes. The office is built on trust and a passionate work ethic.

SP: *Leave is not a reward.*

SB: It's not a reward and it's not something that you should feel like you have to work towards. It's a good thing. Someone who works with us has their own business building and designing skate parks in the Middle East, I would much rather support him and get the benefits of having him as part of our team. This experience brings so much to our projects.

SP: *Could you identify any opportunities that have arisen because of your changed work structure or your alternative approach?*

SB: Yes, at the studio we've got our core group of people who are employed, then there's a series of other people who sub contract, and they're from various disciplines: skate park design/ documentation, illustration, horticulture etc. So there are all these other people, that in a typical model you would work with as one company, but this is more about the individual. There's a whole series of people that are self-employed, starting out or in between jobs, and I've really enjoyed working with these wonderful people, having inspiring conversations, having fresh individuals in the office and it being one on one with either myself or other people in the office. Once the project is complete, everyone adds this project to their folio and it helps us all. Again it's just a different way of sharing knowledge that has in turn influenced how we design or how we go about things, and also what we can offer to clients. A lot of positivity has come out of that.

We're working with a landscape architect – Karl Russo in Kilkunda on a project together because he hasn't done play spaces before, and he's a wonderful detail designer, he also fabricates things, so we're sharing our knowledge between each other – a skill swap.

This means that I can share things that we know and he can share things that he knows. It's not this idea of 'I need to be protective of my information', it needs to be far more open and we all need to realise that there's such a risk of us being the generalist, that a way of going about that is to pull in certain people and then you have an expertise that you can share and learn from.

SP: *Could you say that skill sharing has filtered into the projects that you do? Would you like to go through maybe a more recent one?*

SB: A project we could talk about is a volcano playground we're designing in a park with Urban Edge. Urban Edge were engaged to do a regional park in Beveridge, in the middle of a housing estate that they had also been involved in. Instead of doing the playspace themselves they brought us in to design and document the playspace. This means there are two different landscape architects working on it side by side, and it means that we have more time to apply to the creativity of the play space and they have more time to do the broader landscape. So from a design perspective, it will be two very different approaches side by side. I can't wait to see it in a month or two when it's complete.

SP: *That's very interesting. Thank you so much, I think we can end we can end that one there. unless there's anything else?*

SB: An additional thought, related to your question about political agendas and a friction, the types of projects that we are involved in and the types of projects that are funded could do with a little shake up.

There is so much opportunity to use design as a tool for a broader range of people. Such as creating gardens for commission flats, or applying a landscape budget to women's refuge centres, these are the people that need healing gardens and safe spaces the most. We're doing a project at the moment for an asylum seeker medical centre that a doctor has set up of his own accord, because there's no public funding associated with that type of building, and everyone whose working on it, is doing it predominantly pro bono. So currently, there's a disjunct between who needs certain types of public space and who actually benefits from it.

EMMA MENDEL

Beyond the Orthographic: New models for representing cultural practices

Representing Indigenous knowledge. 2018. University of Virginia, School of Architecture, Emma Mendel, Image by Cong Nie

If, as James Corner says, 'Landscapes are ... the inevitable result of cultural interpretation and the accumulation of representational sediments over time'[1], how do we continue to layer these cultural interpretations into our contemporary methods and tools of design? We have promoted dominant forms of knowledge in our representations of landscape, studied complex ecological and infrastructural systems with carefully predicted outcomes, to ultimately simplify and make evident the process by which we design the built environment. But what about the unidentified, the unseen and the hidden? It is at this juncture that landscapes' potential can be exposed, at the fulcrum of the environment, as an evolved community and as abstracted culture.

There has been a loss in how we enable imagination and reimagination in design due to an over dependence on allied disciplines, mainly stemming from a Euro-Western framework, that gives birth to blind spots. Blind spots, in this sense, are voids that we have ignored due to the dominant Euro-Western methods that were introduced to us at an early age, and dependent on instructions and definitive answers. In the discipline of landscape architecture today, these blind spots are identifying themselves; our agnostic stance floats them on the surface and our reluctance to take responsibility is compounded by a dependence on designing through the lens of census data, referencing scientific research and quoting policy makers.

If landscape is situated between the abstraction of the engineered and the intensity of the sensorial, representation can give a voice to under-represented perspectives. On the other hand, representational methods that address design rooted in cultural dependencies lack a similar breadth of design tools. Design tools have provided increasing sophistication in mapping, drawing and modelling known scenarios, which has allowed for precision in quantifying landscape to inform predictions. However, what is local or Indigenous is suppressed or ignored and the outcome lacks nuance, with consequences for the advancement of other forms of knowledge.

Julia Watson, Adjunct Professor in Urban Planning at Columbia University, has been documenting and cataloguing Indigenous infrastructures.[2] Her forthcoming book aims to classify the many types of Indigenous infrastructures scattered across our planet, showcasing their function and material use. This exciting body of research is much needed in the profession.

But with the publication of such examples, we must also acknowledge what such information does to under-represented communities within a dominant Euro-Western framework. To this point, we must be responsible with forms of representation and methods of documenting as the publicisation of it yields control and power. This consideration is pertinent, especially in the context of climate change. It is those who are currently the most abstracted from the Euro-Western framework of knowledge generation and documentation that set to experience climate change's effects in its most extreme and grotesque forms.[3]

Against such cataclysmic pressures, which will affect thousands if not millions, we must be strategic and mindful of the specificity of such intelligences. I mention intelligence here, not knowledge, as the two cannot be conflated. Intelligence is 'the ability to acquire and apply knowledge and skills'. Alternatively, knowledge can be understood as information which is gained through experience or is taught; the theoretical or practical understanding of a subject. All this is to say that context is meaningful, it nurtures; it requires cultural infrastructures and practices to be readapted rather than transplanted.

The following documents a seminar I taught. It was structured around three exercises that tested, analysed and unpacked contemporary forms of representation, which ultimately lead to discovering a series of "blind spots" in the agency of the designer and representation.

Blind spots

'Locating the self is a tactic common to feminist methodologies to acknowledge that knowledge comes from somewhere and is, therefore, bound up in power relations'.[4] This set the tone for the seminar. Students were tasked to visually represent their own knowledge, situating it within formative events. In this exercise, students defined knowledge in their own terms, identifying its origins and sources. The challenge was made evident when students began to use scientific, quantitative mappings to represent how their own knowledge was conceived: what is its essence (example, oral, sacred); its dimensions (example, proportions, spatiality); its position; and its temporality, cycles and narratives. In endeavouring to draw knowledge, students mapped pseudo-imaginary geographic locations, inventing nuanced scales, connections and timelines. This, in turn, drove discussions on representations from personal perspectives and what is deemed knowledge worthy of representing.

The exercise aligned with the reading of *The Cosmopolitical Proposal*, written by the scientific philosopher Isabelle Stengers. In the text, Stengers begins by defining the cosmopolitical proposal as, 'open to misunderstanding, liable to the Kantian temptation of inferring that politics should aim at allowing a "cosmos," a "good common world" to exist – while the idea is precisely to slow down the construction of this common world, to create a space for hesitation regarding what it means to say "good"'. She then goes on to compare the negligence of other forms of knowledge to "the idiot." The idiot in the ancient Greek sense was someone who didn't speak the Greek language 'and was therefore cut off from the civilized community'.[5]

The Euro-Western framework

The first exercise challenged what forms of knowledge are promoted in design representation. The second assignment called upon students to illustrate a cultural practice through the orthographic projection, precisely presenting the quantitative experience. The drawings produced clarity, order and simplification, but lacked power in expressing the complexity and nuance of an Indigenous knowledge, spatial practice and daily routine. Essentially, landscape cannot simply be 'an ameliorative or restorative practice, but is more precisely a figurative and representational art, providing culture with a sense of existential orientation through the construction of a built symbolic environment'.[6]

In the decision over what is drawn and not drawn in a representation of a cultural practice, the epistemological-ontological divide, presents itself as 'one's perception of the world as being distinct from what is in the world, or what constitutes it'.[7]

In Velez's project, she focused on First Nations communities along Washington and British Columbia, mapping the Coast Salish language and territories with environmental threats. Limitations in the plan drawings lead to reductive representations that were unable to elicit the innate relationship between the community and land.

Representing place-thought

'The "real architecture" only exists in the drawings. The "real building" exists outside the drawing. The difference here is that "architecture" and "building" are not the same'.[8]

The final exercise investigates and develops novel modes of representation with analogue modelling, drawing and other forms of depiction. Three overarching categories of blind spots were challenged: time, perspective and hierarchy. Students were introduced to cosmological and philosophical frameworks such as the Anishinaabe peoples' depiction and understanding of land and dirt. 'In this relationship with dirt, humans are responsible to land the way an owner might be responsible for a pet. This type of dirt is not First Woman; it is a plaything asking for attention'.[9]

'Place-Thought is the non-distinctive space where place and thought were never separated because they never could or can be separated. Place-Thought is based upon the premise that land is alive and thinking and that humans and non-humans derive agency through the extensions of these thoughts'.

It was at this stage in the seminar that students were able to begin to touch upon such complexities. 'As David Turnbull suggests, "Knowledge is performative. In the act of producing knowledge, we create space"'.[10] These potentials were exhibited and experienced through the reinventive taxonomy of relationships. That being said, the bigger issue is in the gap between the design drawing and more personal forms of representation. To avoid the trappings of cultural appropriation, the class was structured to hopefully develop a precision in the agency of representing other forms of knowledge. Ultimately the biggest challenge of the class was students delving into an esoteric process versus being more rigorous in breaking conventions in a constructive way.

From the actual to the possible

The class ultimately exposed the power of representation as a vehicle to present other forms of knowledge, ultimately adding alternative possibilities in the process of design. This method revealed nuanced methodologies and processes, further catapulting projects to novel modes of thinking and designing. The representations and processes transcend the preconceived associations of intelligence in order to conceptualise it as a set of cultural understandings that are embedded within the structural, experiential and tectonic formation of an urban and contemporary environment. Representing networks, contexts and relationships has the capability of driving cultural meaning.

If landscape is situated between the abstraction of the engineered and the intensity of the sensorial, representation can give a voice to under-represented perspectives. On the other hand, representational methods that address design rooted in cultural dependencies lack a similar breadth of design tools. As we approach the ever more complex challenge of survival on our planet, it is crucial to push for nuanced forms of representation that require methodologies focused on strengthening microcosmic relationships between community, land and infrastructure, while creating a platform for non-Euro-Western frameworks.

As philosopher of science Stengers expressed, 'Memory or experience can never be built up if the concern for relevance does not predominate'[11]. In her statement she is not advocating for the rejection of the neutrality of science, but highlighting that without laboratories, experiments and researchers we would not be able to imagine and discover new methodologies without consequence.

FeiFan Zhang

NO MAN'S LAND

The phrase "no man's land" is often understood as undetermined territory that stays unoccupied and is suffused with fear and uncertainty. I am interested in representing how structured intentions coincide with perplexing functions that exist in the urban landscape, as well as how those uncertain functions impact the human experience.

No Man's Land is an exploration of irresolvable and un-relatable spaces – the dark cavities that populate the city. My interest in this subject began when I was living in Beijing and witnessed its renovation and the resultant ambiguities of land usage. When I moved to Chicago in 2015, I was intrigued by similar issues, and I believe my explorations could have been undertaken in any number of urban settings.

Employing spatial relations of elements, natural and artificial light, as well as colour and weather conditions in large scale prints, I emphasise the characters of inaccessibility, uncertainty, deficiency, even brutality, of these spaces. Ultimately, the work speaks to the tenuous relationship we have with the built environment and our attempts to reconcile the often dysfunctional elements within the urban landscape.

What are you supposed to do with this landscape?

What are you expected to do while you are there?

Why are you expected to be there?

Why would you be there?

For these urban spaces the answer seems to be welcoming yet also rejecting (or trapping). My photographs welcome you with a potential invite to "enter" and interact. The larger structures form the orient of functionality and the smaller elements seems to serve a purpose for that. Yet, you are psychologically confused and physically uncomfortable. By revealing the way small-scale elements and large-scale structures interact, my photographs create landscapes that feel collaged. Our experience for landscapes, like this, is fragmentary rather than linear. As a result, you feel trapped and your hope for interaction with the urban space is unfulfilled.

This landscape is constantly shaped by idealism and imposition.

Where would you choose to go, and what would you choose to do?

Does it look like it is designed for you?

Most of all, what looks human to you?

Meremiya Hussein

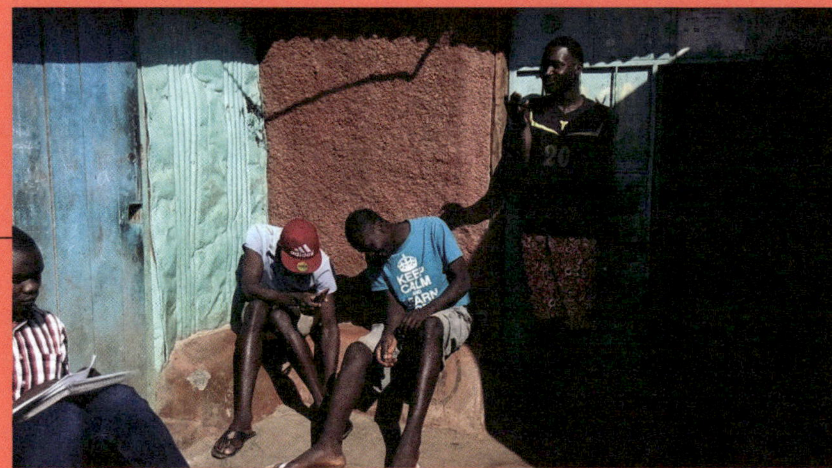

Young people in Kibera hanging out at a Base.
Image credit Pascal Kipkemboi, 2017

Niko Base. This is a *Sheng*[1] phrase, often heard among Nairobi's lower class youth, which loosely translates to: 'I'm at the hangout'. Hangout spaces, often referred to as "the Base", are platforms for the continuous moulding of *Sheng*, a slang that is widely used in Nairobi and consists of mixed English, Swahili and vernacular language. *Sheng* is, arguably, the determinant of authentic Nairobi culture. This article intends to redirect perceptions around the Base as a valid public space by exploring its importance to cultural contribution through language in Nairobi.

Nairobi was planned in the nineteenth century along racial segregation lines, both for housing and employment.[2] The city began as a colonial capital to which native Africans migrated from various parts of the country, as a labour force. These workers found themselves living in settlements with heterogeneous tribal compositions. Efforts to improve communication between these groups, and the rise of a Nairobi culture, gave birth to *Sheng*. This deduction is supported in a study by Iraki[3] where he determines that culture is a product of the human mind and it is defined, propagated and sustained through language. Although the relationship between language and culture is indisputably symbiotic, language serves as an expression of culture without being entirely synonymous with it. Small scale public spaces in Nairobi's informal settlements are cradles for Nairobi culture, where both language and culture evolve with changing times and current affairs.

Post-independence, a relaxation of policies that curtailed migration into Nairobi, such as the Native Registration Amendment Ordinance of 1920[4], resulted in a population surge. This saw Nairobi's population grow from 11,512 people in 1906 to 827,755 people in 1979.[5] Poor planning and unprecedented population growth led to an influx of slums. Up until 2000, when Kenya adopted the Millenium Development Goals (MDGs), the dominant form of slum eradication was forced evictions and razing of these settlements. Over the years, Kenya has tried and tested other methods, like site and settlement schemes, while NGOs have made some headway with engaging the individual community level, and supporting the formation of community-based organisations (CBOs) to represent and strengthen the voice of the poor.[6]

However, all these interventions have focused on housing and infrastructure, without consideration for the broader social and economic needs of low-income communities, resulting in lopsided development. The needs of the residents have generally been oversimplified, resulting in small scale efforts being isolated and ineffective in regard to broader, long-term impacts.[7] As highlighted above, socio-economic needs in informal settlements are pegged on the Base. The Base is more often than not a derelict space, usually an abandoned structure, or simply a bunch of rubber tyres by the roadside, where youth gather to talk, smoke, and share experiences. Although the perception is that it's a place where rowdy unemployed youths pass time, in reality it is where ideas originate, opportunity is sought, psychological help is offered

Communities using rehabilitated public spaces. Public Space Project 10, Andolo bench and shade structure, part of the Kibera Public Space Project. Image credit Pascal Kipkemboi, 2019

and a cultural identity is formed. For communities in informal settlements, it serves as a more than a public space. It is a public space that is productive, both socially and economically. Through networking of these spaces it is possible to create a large-scale effect, which can catalyse development in informal settlements.

Given the fact that urban youth make up the majority of Nairobi's population, and most (sixty to seventy per cent) of Nairobi's inhabitants live in informal settlements[8], planning for public spaces is serving an elite minority if efforts and resources are not directed towards the majority of Nairobi's inhabitants. Although the Nairobi county government has made strides towards developing these spaces - most recently in partnership with the Public Space Network, and an undertaking of a city-wide inventory and assessment of public spaces with UN-Habitat and the Technical University of Kenya[9] - it still excludes slum Bases. This exclusion translates to discounting those young people living in informal settlements, and destroying an incubator of Nairobi's culture where a homogenous and tolerant society in rough environments is anchored.

Nonprofit organisations like KDI (Kounkuey Design Initiative) are championing the protection of such spaces. KDI's solution lies in making these spaces productive, so that they serve both social and economic needs. They work with community groups who are expected to manage these productive public spaces, and ensure their productivity through economic activities carried out in these spaces.

This removes the perception that these Bases are spaces for social ill and transforms them into spaces where young people can be enterprising and serve their communities through small scale social entrepreneurship. In the context of KDI's work in Kenya, neighbourhood-scale projects improve physical and social conditions by reclaiming "leftover" waste spaces. However, these spaces are envisioned from the outset as components of a future network, through strategic selection and coordination of project sites. A network of residents and institutional collaborators grows in tandem with the physical network and builds new economies, social safety nets and political capital at the scale of the site, settlement and beyond.

KDI Kenya has made significant strides since 2006, when six students from Harvard University's Design School first travelled to Kibera, an informal settlement in Kenya. It has worked with residents to design and activate a network of productive public spaces that could meet their physical, social and economic needs. The Kibera Public Space Project network has transformed polluted, unsafe sites into vibrant assets, building community resilience and capacity while remediating the entire watershed. Women and youth in particular benefit from income-generating opportunities and increased security. Together, the sites anchor a network of leaders who share knowledge and skills to effect widespread change. The network continues to grow and build resilience across the settlement today.[10]

Chloe **Sterland**

Artwork by Alice Coates

U B E R

'You know, I just tell the girls, "you're really beautiful, but I can't have sex with you"'.

There are still thirteen minutes left of this Uber ride. I fumble for a response that will make the rest of the trip bearable and to keep my Uber rating above 4.84. My driver is regaling me with stories about all the female passengers he rejects, glancing at me in the rear-view mirror as he speaks, his snapback casting shadows over his eyes. I fiddle with my coat buttons. He warns me about the current situation of the Uber driver – passenger intercourse. He tells me that sometimes drunk girls ask Uber drivers to have sex with them. And then the next day report it as rape. So that's why he has a 'no sex with Uber customers policy'. Even though girls ask him for it. A lot, by the sounds of it.

It's odd to miss public transport. I miss the anonymity. I catch the bus to university, a journey that provides me with endless entertainment: making eye contact with cute guys, being unsure about whether the eye-contact occurred because I was staring at their face; or because our eyes were drawn together by some cosmic force; the little interactions with strangers sitting next to me, gathering your bag onto your lap to signal you have to get off, maybe you smile at them, maybe they smile back. For me, these small occurrences are where a lot of the joy of public life happens, in these moments in between our busy schedules that we can't plan, organise or control. Whether it be on a street or bus or with the person behind the counter at a local cafe. The way we can experience the unexpected or the new: meeting new people, smiling at strangers, dramatic eye contact with passing potential soulmates, people watching, animal watching, or a kooky looking house.

My Uber driver told me he 'was a troll' within the first few minutes of the ride. I keep this in mind when responding to anything he says. I continue with my usual designated Uber chit chat. 'Has it been a busy night?', 'What time did you start?', 'Being an Uber driver must be so great, you get to be your own boss?'. But now I wonder what 'being your own boss' means? Does this mean you can talk about sex with customers? Accountability is blurred with Uber.

Uber is used for a number of reasons. Convenience, public transport taking too long, or because, especially for women, it's seen as safer than the alternative – safer than walking six minutes home from the bus stop. Or twenty from the tram. Or through the creepy area around a seemingly abandoned train station. Minimising risk is something women do daily; when choosing to take Uber instead of public transport, when going to and from the grocery store. We make certain choices, to not go down a street because it's too dark, or because we were cat-called there once. We create paths of avoidance within our cities – areas women don't go in fear of harassment. When we discuss safety, especially in relation to women, it's often in opposition to risk – a utopian risk free world, where women aren't sexually assaulted or harassed. But we don't live in a utopic world, so in today's society this thinking encourages retorts like women shouldn't be in public places at night. Because now they're not at risk. Now they're safe, right? This mindset drives women out of public spaces and can even be seen in how we design solutions. Instead of re-designing a service or environment as a whole, we isolate the only slightly "controllable" aspect of the situation – women – and develop band-aid solutions. The pink "women only" carriages in Tokyo are an apt example of this. Equal access to public space is, therefore, not just discouraged by the societal rhetoric around women and safety, but also by design.

In a moment of poor judgement, I bring up Shebah, the female only rideshare. He says he thinks it's sexist to men. I want to say 'I didn't realise men felt uncomfortable taking Uber, or scared for their safety'. But I don't. I've developed a kind of mantra in my head. It consists of 'he's a troll' over and over again. I say, 'well at least they feel safer'. He says 'yeah well it's also more expensive, but I guess you can't put a price on safety'.

I recently went to a panel discussion where the CEO of Shebah spoke. She started her talk with statistics on how much more money women spend going to a football game, because we take more private transport than men. She then continued to talk about her company, which ironically charges women more than Uber. I understand why it charges more (my dad drew a supply and demand graph in the air as we had dinner the other night, as I vehemently said 'that's not my point!'), and it's not the main reason I'm sceptical about services like Shebah. I'm sceptical about Shebah because I'm worried about the message it produces, similar to women-only carriages. Our behaviour is changed, rather than the perpetrators', or existing structures. I take public transport because it's safer than walking. And then I choose Uber because it's safer than public transport. Then Shebah because it's safer than Uber (the "safer" I get, the more I seem to pay...). And all of this results in less and less women inhabiting public space. What if, instead of creating services and designs to encourage women to avoid public places, we focused on how to make these spaces areas that women would want to dwell? I'm emphatically echoing Shilpa Phadke's[1] call of comfort:

> One possible way to radicalise the demand for greater access to public space is to forsake the category of 'safety' and to focus instead on 'comfort'...

Comfort suggests not just the absence of violence, but an active sense of belonging.

Instead of focusing on creating alternative services we should analyse and re-design the existing frameworks. In Toronto they added a bus program where at night people can request stops in between official bus stops, giving targeted people agency and choice. Allowing people to get off when they choose takes into account the different experiences of using public transport – responding to the fear that may exist between the bus stop and the home. Designers, urban planners, architects and problem solvers need to go through each iteration of that journey, right down to how we can make the journey out of a train station more comfortable; to ensure that while we as a wider society chip away at changing how we view women and men, the infrastructure supports the idea that everyone should have equal access to, and comfort in, public space.

But, for now, I will sit uncomfortably in the Uber, fidgeting with my coat buttons. When Mum says things such as, 'Did you hear about that thing on the news? Now I've got to worry about you taking Ubers!', I'll get annoyed at her for feeding the fear, the fear that has been force-fed to me by movies, the media, and politicians my whole life. But I'll still consider setting my home address on the Uber app to a few houses down from mine, so the driver doesn't know exactly where I live.

References

Danielle Toronyi

[1] ET Parner, DE. Schendel, and P Thorsen, 'Autism Prevalence Trends Over Time in Denmark: Changes in Prevalence and Age at Diagnosis', *Archives of Pediatrics and Adolescent Medicine*, vol. 162, no. 12, 2008, pp. 1150-1156.

[2] E Gomes, et al., 'Auditory Hypersensitivity in Children and Teenagers with Autistic Spectrum Disorder', *Arquivos de Neuro-psiquiatria*, vol. 62, no. 3b, 2004, pp. 797-801.

[3] N Boddaert, 'Perception of Complex Sounds in Autism: Abnormal Auditory Cortical Processing in Children', *American Journal of Psychiatry*, vol. 161, no. 11, 2004, pp. 2117-2120.

[4] M Mostafa, 'Architecture for Autism: Built Environment Performance in Accordance to the Autism ASPECTSS™ Design Index', *Design Principles and Practices*, vol. 8 no. 1, 2015, pp. 55-71.

[5] M Kusenbach, 'Street Phenomenology: The Go-Along as Ethnographic Research Tool', *Ethnography*, vol. 4, no. 3, 2003, pp. 455–485.

[6] R Longhurst, E Ho and L Johnston, 'Using the Body as an Instrument of Research: Kimchi and Pavlova', *Area*, vol. 40, no. 2, 2008, pp. 208–217.

[7] PC Adams, 'Peripatetic imagery and peripatetic sense of place', in P.C. Adams, S. Hoelscher and K.E. Till (eds.), *Textures of Place: Exploring Humanist Geographies*, Minneapolis, University of Minneapolis Press, 2001, pp. 186-206.

[8] L Halprin, *The RSVP Cycles: Creative Processes in the Human Environment*, n.p. George Braziller, 1970, n.p.

Éloïse Choquette

[1] M Brown, 'Revived: the 1930s London Gay Members' Club Raided by Police', *The Guardian*, 27 February 2017, http://www.theguardian.com/culture/2017/feb/27/revived-1930slondon- gay-members-club-caravan-club-raided-by-police, (accessed 15 March 2017).

[2] H Forsythe, *Exploring LGBTQ Spaces and Places in History*, The National Archives, blog. nationalarchives.gov.uk/blog/exploring-lgbtq-spaces-places-history/ (accessed 15 March 2017).

[3] A Lorde, 'The Master's Tools Will Never Dismantle The Master's House,' in Sister Outsider: Essays and Speeches, Trumansburg, New York: Crossing Press, 1984, pp. 110–114.

Sarah Dooling

[1] L Bliss, 'The High Line's next balancing act', *City Lab*, 7 February 2017, https://www.citylab.com/solutions/2017/02/the-high-lines-next-balancing-act-fair-and-affordable-development/515391/, (Accessed 10 February 2019).

Yazid Ninsalam & Michaela Prescott

[1] C Freund and M Ruta, 'Belt and Road Initiative', World Bank, 2018, https://www.worldbank.org/en/topic/regional-integration/brief/belt-and-road-initiative, (accessed 05 June 2019).

[2] W Yi, 'The Belt and Road Initiative Is Not a "Marshall Plan" but a Vivid Practice of Jointly Building a Community with a Shared Future for Mankind', *Ministry of Foreign Affairs, the People's Republic of China*, 2018, https://www.fmprc.gov.cn/mfa_eng/zxxx_662805/t1588358.shtml, (accessed 05 June 2019).

[3] J Hurley et al., 'Examining the Debt Implications of the Belt and Road Initiative from a Policy Perspective', DC, *Center for Global Development*. Https://Www.Cgdev.Org/Publication/Exam, 2018, (accessed 05 June 2019).

[4] S Jayawardana, 'Clashes Erupt as Govt Launches Southern Development Projects', *Sunday Times*, 2017, http://www.sundaytimes.lk/170108/news/clashes-erupt-as-govt-launches-southern-development-projects-223369.html, (accessed 05 June 2019).

[5] J Griffiths, 'Just What Is This One Belt, One Road Thing Anyway?,' CNN, 12 May 2017, https://edition.cnn.com/2017/05/11/asia/china-one-belt-one-road-explainer/index.html, (accessed 05 June 2019).

[6] In its own right, the very euphemism of the 'white elephant' in the context of this discussion seems appropriate. Across Southeast Asia – in spite of political differences – white elephants are perceived not just as symbols, but functional baubles promoting national wellbeing and stability. In modern English the expression is used to describe an extremely expensive construction project that fails to deliver on its function or becomes very costly to maintain. According to legend, the king of Siam (now Thailand) would gift white elephants to those whom he disliked hoping that the high handling cost would bankrupt them. It would have been a gross insult to decline such a gift.

[7] E Oh, 'Sasaki's "Forest City" Master Plan in Iskandar Malaysia Stretches Across 4 Islands', *ArchDaily*, 2 February 2016, https://www.archdaily.com/781247/sasakis-forest-city-master-plan-in-iskandar-malaysia-stretches-across-4-islands, (accessed 05 June 2019).

[8] Dr Nik & Associates SDN. BHD., 'Detailed Environmental Impact Assessment (DEIA) for the Proposed Forest City Island Reclamation & Mixed Development, Johor', (Johor, Malaysia, 2014).

[9] S Ourbis and A Shaw, 'Malaysia's Forest City and the Damage Done', *The Diplomat*, 30 August 2017, https://thediplomat.com/2017/08/malaysias-forest-city-and-the-damage-done/ (accessed 05 June 2019).

[10] S Rahman, 'Johor's Forest City Faces Critical Challenges', *ISEAS – Yusof Ishak Institute, Singapore*, 2017, no. 3, pp. 1–37.

[11] S Zhen, 'Country Garden Pledges Refund for Forest City Buyers Caught in Beijing's Crackdown on Capital Outflows', *South China Morning Post*, 5 April 2017, https://www.scmp.com/business/companies/article/2084744/country-garden-pledges-refund-forest-city-buyers-caught-beijings%0A, (accessed 05 June 2019).

[12] J Sipalan, 'Dr M: Foreigners Cannot Buy Residential Units in Forest City', *The Star*, 27 August 2018, https://www.thestar.com.my/business/business-news/2018/08/27/malaysia-says-forest-city-project-off-limits-to-foreign-buyers/#UiOSLwZql8CqoZ9l.99, (accessed 05 June 2019).

[13] S Strangio, 'Malaysia Wrestles With Beijing's One Belt One Road Bonanza', *Forbes Asia*, 29 November 2017, https://www.forbes.com/sites/forbesasia/2017/11/29/malaysia-my-second-home/#5240d9677bda , (accessed 05 June 2019).

[14] K Schneider, 'A Civic Outcry in Malaysia Forces a Chinese Builder to Live up to Its Eco-Friendly Tag', Mongabay Series: Southeast Asian Infrastructure, *Mongabay*, 5 September 2018, https://news.mongabay.com/2018/09/a-civic-outcry-in-malaysia-forces-a-chinese-builder-to-live-up-to-its-eco-friendly-tag/, (accessed 05 June 2019).

Roberto Boettger

[1] "Separation" derives from Karl Marx's concept of primitive accumulation. For Marx, it is the precondition for the accumulation of capital where an 'original' appropriation of wealth occurs through 'direct extra-economical forces,' such as physical violence or, in this case, legislation. See K Marx, 'Part Eight: So-Called Primitive Accumulation', *Capital Volume 1*, trans. Ben Fowkes, London, Penguin Books, [1867] 1979.

[2] Conservation is seen here as the impossibility of "use". As a concept, it is analogous to Giorgio Agamben's notion of "museification". See G Agamben, "In Praise of Profanation", in *Profanations*, New York, Zone Books, 2017, p. 83.

Ed Kermode & Dan Parker

[1] M Murray, *The Urbanism of Exception: The Dynamics of Global City Building in the Twenty-First Century*, Cambridge University Press, 2017.

[2] C Mills, *Biopolitics*, New York, NY, Routledge, 2017.

[3] M Laurence, *Biopolitics and State Regulation of Human Life*, Oxford University Press, 2016.

[4] D Fernández, and A. Schwabe, 'Offsetted', *Cooking Sections*, <http://www.cooking-sections.com/Offsetted>, (accessed 13 May 2019).

[5] M Trotter, 'Sanford Kwinter & Marrikka Trotter: On Liveliness', <https://www.youtube.com/watch?v=7ed7JtoWhdM&t=1952s>, (accessed 13 May 2019).

Bede Brennan & Minna Leunig

[1] AL Tsing, *The Mushroom at the End of the World*, Princeton University Press, 2015.

[2] K Anderson, 'Culture and Nature at the Adelaide Zoo: At the Frontiers of 'Human' Geography', *Transactions of the Institute of British Geographers*, 1995, vol. 20, no. 3, pp. 275–294.

[3] V Plumwood, *Feminism and the Mastery of Nature*, London, Routledge, 1993.

[4] N Castree, 'Nature is dead! Long live nature!' *Environment and Planning*, 2004, vol. 36, pp. 191–194.

[5] Ibid.

[6] M Pollan, *Second Nature: A Gardeners Education*, London, Harper Publishing, 1992.

[7] W McLennan, 'In Australia, a sewage facility is now one of the world's greatest bird habitats', *Foreground*, 30 Jan 2019, www.foreground.com.au/environment/industrial-ecology-werribee-western-treatment-plant/ (accessed 5 May 2019).

[8] V Plumwood, 'Shadow Places and the Politics of Dwelling'. *Australian Humanities Review*, ANU Press, 2008, vol.44,

[9] A Blechman, *Pigeons: The Fascinating Saga of the World's Most Revered and Reviled Bird*, Brisbane, University of Queensland Press, 2006.

[10] M Thomson, 'Placing the wild in the city: "thinking with" Melbournes' Bats', *Society & Animals*, 2007, vol. 15, pp.79–95.

[11] R. Conniff, 'Urban Nature: How to Foster Biodiversity in World's Cities', *Yale Environment 360*, 6 January 2019, <https://e360.yale.edu/features/urban_nature_how_to_foster_biodiversity_in_worlds_cities>, (accessed 5 May 2019).

[12] Ibid.

[13] K Soanes and P Lentini, 'When cities are the Last Chance for Saving Species', *Frontiers in Ecology and the Environment*, Ecological Society of America, 2019, vol. 17, no. 4, pp. 225–231.

[14] N Thrift, 'From Born to Made: Technology, Biology and Space', in Philo, C (ed), *Theory and Methods: Critical Essays in Human Geography*, London, Routledge, 2017.

[15] Ibid.

[16] Ibid. 11.

[17] D Abrams, *Spell of the Sensuous: Perception and Language in a More Than Human World*, London, Vintage, 1996.

[18] Ibid.

Lewis McNeice

[1] International Federation of Red Cross and Red Crescent Societies, *World Disaster Report, Leaving No-one Behind*, 2018, https://media.ifrc.org/ifrc/world-disaster-report-2018/, (accessed 05 June 2019).

[2] P Bellegarde-Smith, 'A Man-Made Disaster: The Earthquake of January 12, 2010 – a Haitian Perspective', *Journal of Black Studies*, vol. 42, no. 2, 2011, pp. 264-275.

[3] C. Hartman and GD Squires, *There is No Such Thing as a Natural Disaster: Race, Class and Hurricane Katrina*, New York and London, Routledge, 2008, pp. 1-3.

[4] D Barton, 2017. *Disaster in Relation to Attachment, Loss, Grief and Recovery: The Marysville Experience*, Ph.D. diss., Melbourne, RMIT University, 2017, https://researchbank.rmit.edu.au/eserv/rmit:162288/Barton.pdf, (accessed 17 August 2019).

[5] Regional Australia Institute, *From Disaster To Renewal: The Centrality of Business Recovery to Community Resilience*, Canberra, ACT, Regional Australia Institute, 2013.

[6] B Pease, Privileged Irresponsibility and Global Warming, 2018, https://www.youtube.com/watch?time_continue=119&v=OhPvzzpSqG4, (accessed 23 September 2018).

Sofija Kaljević

[1] A Hauser, *The Philosophy of Art History*, New York, Routledge, 2018.

[2] M Stierli and V Kulić, eds, *Toward a Concrete Utopia: Architecture in Yugoslavia, 1948–1980*, New York, The Museum of Modern Art, *2018*.

[3] Ibid. 7.

[4] M Stierli, 'Networks and Crossroads: The Architecture of Socialist Yugoslavia as a Laboratory of Globalization in the Cold War,' in *Toward a Concrete Utopia: Architecture in Yugoslavia, 1948–1980*, New York, The Museum of Modern Art, 2018.

[5] V Kulić, 'Building Brotherhood and Unity: Architecture and Federalism in Socialist Yugoslavia,' in *Toward a Concrete Utopia: Architecture in Yugoslavia, 1948–1980*, New York, The Museum of Modern Art, 2018, p. 42.

[6] Ibid.

[7] M Mrduljaš, 'Architecture for a Self-Managing Socialism,' in *Toward a Concrete Utopia: Architecture in Yugoslavia, 1948–1980*, New York, The Museum of Modern Art, 2018, p. 42.

[8] Ibid., 42.

[9] No author. 'Zakljucci 1. Jugoslavenskog Savjetovanja o Stambenoj Izgradnji i Stanovanju i Gradovima,' *Covjek i Prostor*, vol. 52, 1956, pp. 1-8.

[10] M Mrduljaš, 'Architecture for a Self-Managing Socialism,' in *Toward a Concrete Utopia: Architecture in Yugoslavia, 1948–1980*, New York, The Museum of Modern Art, 2018, p. 45.

[11] Examples: Housing Blocks of New Begrade, Serbia, and Brace Broznan building block, Split, Croatia.

[12] M Mrduljaš, 'Architecture for a Self-Managing Socialism,' in *Toward a Concrete Utopia: Architecture in Yugoslavia, 1948–1980*, New York, The Museum of Modern Art, 2018, p. 50.

[13] Examples: S Kaljević, 'Exploring Memory of Place and Place Identity through Narrative Inquiry: A Study of Partisans' Square in Uzice, Serbia', PhD diss., West Virginia University, 2018.

[14] M Mrduljaš, 'Architecture for a Self-Managing Socialism,' in *Toward a Concrete Utopia: Architecture in Yugoslavia, 1948–1980*, New York, The Museum of Modern Art, 2018, p. 53.

[15] Ibid., 46.

[16] V Kulić, 'Building Brotherhood and Unity: Architecture and Federalism in Socialist Yugoslavia,' In *Toward a Concrete Utopia: Architecture in Yugoslavia, 1948–1980*, New York, The Museum of Modern Art, p. 34.

[17] Ibid., 33.

[18] H Lefebvre, *Le Droit a la Ville*, Paris, Anthropos, 1968.

[19] D Harvey, *Rebel Cities: From the Right to the City to the Urban Revolution*. London, Verso Books, 2012.

[20] S Zuboff, *The Age of Surveillance Capitalism: The Fight for a Human Future at the New Frontier of Power*, New York, Public Affairs, 2019.

[21] Ibid., 228.

[22] K Marx, *Capital Volume 1*, London, Penguin Classics, 2011.

[23] K McWhirter, 'Hudson Yards was not Inevitable', *Failed Architecture*, https://failedarchitecture.com/hudson-yards-was-not-inevitable/, (accessed 11 May 2019).

[24] D Harvey, 'Erosion of Consumer Choices', *Anti-Capitalist* Chronicles [Podcast], https://podcasts.apple.com/us/podcast/erosion-of-consumer-choices/id1442025854?i=1000436392025, (accessed 2 May 2019).

[25] *Toward Concrete Utopia: Architecture in Yugoslavia 1948–1980*, The Museum of Modern Art, New York, July 2018-January 2019.

Paige Anderson

[1] P Miao, (ed.), *Public Places in Asia Pacific Cities*, Dordrecht, Netherlands, Kluwer Academic Publishers, 2001.

[2] K Cheng, '4 Passengers per Square Meter: New Report Shows TR Overcrowding during Morning Rush', *Hong Kong Free Press*, 13 April 2016.

[3] LC Delmendo, 'Investment Analysis of Hong Kong Real Estate Market', *Global Property Guide*, 6 March 2019, https://www.globalpropertyguide.com/Asia/Hong-Kong/Price- History, (Accessed 21 March, 2016).

[4] L Kuo, 'A Brief History of Hong Kong's 30-Year Fight for Democracy', *Quartz* (blog), http://qz.com/297970/a-brief-history-of-hong-kongs-30-year-fight-for- democracy/.

[5] M Wark, *Virtual Geography*, Indiana University Press, 1994, p. 114.

[6] FX Pasquier, [interviewed by the author] 'Admiralty and the Umbrella Movement', 26 May 2015.

[7] *Hong Kong Silenced*, [Documentary], Tse Sky, VICE News, 2015, https://news.vice.com/video/hong-kong-silenced, (accessed 21 March 2016).

[8] *Riots, Unrest, and the Umbrella Movement: Hong Kong Rising* [Documentary], Tse Sky, VICE News, 2014, https://news.vice.com/video/hong-kong-rising, (accessed 21 March 2016).

[9] Parallel Lab, 'Admiralty', Umbrella Movement, 26 September 2014.

[10] M Purcell, 'Excavating Lefebvre: The Right to the City and Its Urban Politics of the Inhabitant' *GeoJournal*, vol. 58, 2003, pp. 99–108.

[11] G Borio and C Wuthrich, *Hong Kong In-Between*, 1st ed., Zurich, Park Books, 2015.

[12] K Savage, *Monument Wars: Washington, D.C., the National Mall, and the Transformation of the Memorial Landscape*, Pittsburgh, PA, University of California Press, n.d.

Emily Schlickman

[1] WH Whyte, *The Social Life of Small Urban Spaces*, New York, Project for Public Spaces, 2001.

Claire Martin

[1] C Goodman-Strauss, 'Revealed: The Insidious Creep of Pseudo-Public Space in London', *The Guardian*, 24 July 2017, https://www.theguardian.com/cities/2017/jul/24/revealed-pseudo-public-space-pops-london-investigation-map, (accessed 21 March 2019).

[2] Charter of Public Space, adopted in Rome, final session of the II Biennial of Public Space, 2013, https://drive.google.com/file/d/0B5-VDOO42qGmQ1lXRFhkaFRLTDA/view, (accessed 21 March 2019).

[3] 'Record $20 Million Gift to Help Finish the High Line Park', *The New York Times*, 26 October 2011, https://www.nytimes.com/2011/10/27/nyregion/20-million-gift-to-high-line-park.html (accessed 21 March 2019).

[4] H Dardick, 'Millennium Park built 'the Chicago Way', *Chicago Tribune*, 13 July 2014, https://www.chicagotribune.com/news/ct-millennium-park-costs-met-20140714-story.html (accessed 21 March 2019).

[5] 'Public Admin Explainer: What is Public Value?', *ANZOG*, https://www.anzsog.edu.au/resource-library/research/what-is-public-value, (accessed 21 March 2019).

[6] F Gaffikin and M Morrisey, *Planning in Divided Cities*, Great Britain, Wiley-Blackwell, 2011.

[7] 'Towards a Collaborative City: the Case for a Melbourne Metropolitan Commission', *The Conversation*, 2016, https://theconversation.com/towards-a-collaborative-city-the-case-for-a-melbourne-metropolitan-commission-57578, (accessed 21 March 2019).

[8] 'London Mayor to Draw Up Charter Regulating Pseudo-public Space', *The Guardian*, 23 November 2017, https://www.theguardian.com/cities/2017/nov/23/london-mayor-charter-pseudo-public-space-sadiq-khan, (accessed 19 March 2019).

[9] 'Community Development Corporations', *Inc*, https://www.inc.com/encyclopedia/community-development-corporations.html (accessed 19 March 2019).

[10] 'Neighbourhood Matching Fund', *City of Vancouver*, https://vancouver.ca/people-programs/neighbourhood-matching-fund.aspx (accessed 12 May 2019).

[11]. Ibid.

Charlie Clemoes

[1] The phrase is variously associated with International Workers of the World organiser "Big Bill" Haywood and architect Berthold Lubetkin.

[2] K Fox-Hodess, 'Is an Injury to One an Injury to All? Some Critical Thoughts on Trade-Union Internationalism Today', *New Politics*, 2016, https://newpol.org/injury-one-injury-all-some-critical-thoughts-trade-union-internationalism-today/, (Accessed 29 May 2019).

[3] J Alimahomed-Wilson, K Fox-Hodess and K Moody, 'Seizing the Chokepoints', *Jacobin*, 2018, https://www.jacobinmag.com/2018/10/choke-points-logistics-industry-organizing-unions, (Accessed 29 May 2019).

[4] J Schreier, 'Inside Rockstar Games' Culture of Crunch' *Kotaku*, 2018, https://kotaku.com/inside-rockstar-games-culture-of-crunch-1829936466, (Accessed 29 May 2019).

[5] B Sinclair, 'Developers drag Rockstar over 100-hour weeks on Red Dead Redemption 2' *Kotaku*, 2018 https://www.gamesindustry.biz/articles/2018-10-15-developers-drag-rockstar-over-100-hour-work-weeks, (Accessed 29 May 2019).

[6] RK Upadhya, 'Tech Workers Against Imperialism', *Medium*, 2018 https://medium.com/tech-workers-coalition/tech-workers-against-imperialism-2d8024e461a7, (Accessed 29 May 2019).

[7] M Weigel, 'Coders of the World, Unite: Can Silcon Valley Workers Curb the Power of Big Tech?', *The Guardian*, 2018 https://www.theguardian.com/news/2017/oct/31/coders-of-the-world-unite-can-silicon-valley-workers-curb-the-power-of-big-tech, (Accessed 29 May 2019).

[8] TWC's recent zine "Tech Won't Build It!" outlines all the campaigns which have emerged from the #TechWontBuildIt protests, in which tech workers have sought to prevent their employers committing to work that is unethical, including employees at Google applying pressure on the company to pulling out of the competition for the US military's Joint Enterprise Defence Infrastructure (JEDI) cloud computing contract. See: Tech Workers Coalition, *Tech Won't Build it: A TWC Reader*, California, 2018, https://www.slideshare.net/PaigePanter/tech-wont-build-it-zine, (Accessed 29 May 2019).

Lois Nguyen

[1] T Shakespeare, 'The Social Model of Disability', in Davis, LJ, *The Disability Studies Reader*, 4th edn., New York, Routledge, 2013, pp. 216.

[2] Ibid.

[3] I Catanese, 'Thomas Lamb, Marc Harrison, Richard Hollerith and the Origins of Universal Design', *Journal of Design History,* vol. 25, no. 2, 2012, pp. 206–7, http://www.jstor.org.proxy.library.cornell.edu/stable/41687795, (accessed 29 May 2019).

[4] A *Hamraie, Building Access: Universal Design and the Politics of Disability*, Minneapolis, University of Minnesota Press, 2017, pp. 33.

[5] JE Weeber, 'Mace, L. Ronald (1942–1998)' in Albrecht, GL (ed), *Encyclopedia of Disability*, . Thousand Oaks, CA, SAGE Publications Inc., 2006, pp. 10481047, https://doi.org/10.1080/17547075.2016.1218714, (accessed 29 May 2019).

[6] Ibid. The Rehabilitation Act 1973, The Fair Housing Amendments Act 1988, and The Americans with Disabilities Act 1990.

[7] Ibid., 4. Also to note, in *Building Access* (175–221), Aimi Hamraie traces the multiple evolutions of universal design from an experimental design process that resisted the normative code-compliant barrier-free design of the sixties and seventies, to a design agenda promoted for its marketing potential and the niche market of the disabled user.

[8] R Mace, 'Universal Design: Barrier-Free Environments for Everyone', *Designers West*, vol. 33, no. 1, 1985, pp. 148, quoted in Hamraie, *Building Access*, p. 181.

[9] R Lusher, and R. Mace, 'Design for Physical and Mental Disabilities', in Wilkes, JA and Packard, RT (eds), *Encyclopedia of Architecture: Design Engineering and Construction*, New York, John Wiley and Sons, 1989, p. 755.

[10] Ibid. 4, pp. 197–198.

[11] Ibid. 4, p. 184.

[12] Ibid. 4, p. 200.

[13] RL Mace, GJ Hardie, and JP Place, (eds), *Accessible Environments: Toward Universal Design*, Raleigh, NC, Center for Accessible Housing, North Carolina State University, 1990, p. 2.

[14] R Mace, 'Universal Design: Barrier-Free Environments for Everyone', *Designers West*, vol. 33, no. 1, 1985, pp. 152, quoted in Hamraie, *Building Access*, p. 181.

[15] Ibid. 4, p. 212.

[16] Ibid. 4, p. 211., Hamraie expands, '...journalists and manufacturers appropriated the term "Universal Design" to brand any form of user-centered design as good design, ranging from disability designs to mere ergonomics'.

[17] Ibid. 4, p. 13.

[18] A Hamraie, 'Universal Design and the Problem of 'Post-Disability' Ideology', *Design and Culture*, vol. 8, no. 3, September 2016, p. 296.

[19] DT Mitchell, and SL Snyder, *Cultural Locations of Disability*, Chicago, University of Chicago Press, 2006, pp. 6–10.

[20] Ibid.4, p. 95.

Brent Greene & Abigail Varney

[1] ABS (Australian Bureau of Statistics), 'Regional Population Growth, Australia, 201718', *ABS*, 2019, https://www.abs.gov.au/ausstats/abs@.nsf/mf/3218.0, (accessed 5 May 2019)

[2] ABS, 'Regional Population Growth, Australia, 201718', *ABS*, 2019, http://www.abs.gov.au/ausstats/abs@.nsf/Latestproducts/3218.0Main%20Features252017-18, (accessed 5 May 2019)

[3] K Dovey, *Fluid City: Transforming Melbourne's Urban Waterfront*, Sydney, University of New South Wales Press, 2005.

Emma Mendel

[1] J Corner, 'Representation and landscape: Drawing and making in the landscape medium', *Word & Image*, vol. 8, no. 3, 1992, pp. 343–208 DOI: 10.1080/02666286.1992.10435840, (accessed 05 May 2019).

[2] J Watson, 'Indigenous infrastructures', *Urban Design @Columbia GSAPP*, 20 April 2018, http://vimeo.com/265830859, (accessed 02/05/2019).

[3] 'How to Think about Global Warming and War: The great job boom', *The Economist*, May 2019, pp. 15-16

[4] J Sundberg, 'Decolonizing posthumanist geographies', *Cultural Geographies*, vol. 21, no. 1, 2014, pp. 31–47.

[5] Ibid.

[6] I Stengers, 'The Cosmopolitical Proposal', in Latour, B And Weibel, P (eds), *Making Things Public*, MIT Press, 2005, pp. 994–1003.

[7] E Haldane, '*The Philisophical Works of Descartes*', Cambridge University Press, 1911.

[8] J Corner, 'Representation and landscape: Drawing and making in the landscape medium', *Word & Image*, vol. 8, no. 3, 1992, pp. 343–208 DOI: 10.1080/02666286.1992.10435840, (accessed 05 May 2019).

[9] P Eisenman, 'Eisenman's Evolution: Architecture, Syntax, and New Subjectivity', [interviewed by Iman Ansari], *Architectural Review*, 26 April 2013, (accessed 05 May 2019).

[10] V Watts, 'Indigenous Place-Thought and Agency Amongst Humans and Non Humans (First Woman and Sky Woman Go On a European World Tour!)', *Decolonization: Indigeneity, Education & Society*, vol. 2, no. 1, 2013, pp. 20–34.

[11] I Stengers, 'The Cosmopolitical Proposal', in Latour, B And Weibel, P (eds), *Making Things Public*, MIT Press, 2005, pp. 994–1003.

Meremiya Hussein

[1] Slang widely spoken in Nairobi; a concoction of English, Swahili and vernacular languages.

[2] C Blevin and J Bouczo, 'Nairobi: A Century of History 1898-1997', *Les Cahiers de l'IFRA* , pp. 50-53.

[3] FK Iraki, 'Language and Culture - A perspective', *Wajibu Journal*, 2017, http://africa.peacelink.org/wajibu/articles/art_4485.html,. (accessed 05 June 2019)

[4] DM Anderson, 'Master and Servant in Colonial Kenya', *The Journal of African History*, vol. 41, no. 3, 2000, pp. 459-485.

[5] W Olima, 'The Conflicts, Shortcomings and Implications of the Urban Land Management System in Kenya', *Habitat International*, vol. 21, no. 3, 1997, pp. 319-331.

[6] R Chambers, 'Going to Scale with Community Led Total Sanitation: Reflections on Experience, Issues and Ways Forward', *Institute of Development Studies Bulletin*, vol. 1, 2009, pp. 1-50.

[7] C Odbert and J Mulligan, 'The Kibera Public Space Project: Participation, Integration and Networked Change', in Hou, J, Spencer, B, Way, T et al (eds), *Now Urbanism: The Future City is Here*, London and New York, Routledge, 2015, pp. 177-192

[8] *Population and Health Dynamics in Nairobi*, African Population Health Research Center, 2012.

[9] C Karisa, *UoN Department of Urban and Regional Planning*, 2016, http://urbanplanning.uonbi.ac.ke/content/nairobi-city-wide-public-space-strategy-validation-workshop-held-15th-march-2016, (Accessed 2 May 2019).

[10] KDI, *Kounkuey.org*, 2012, https://www.kounkuey.org/projects/kibera_public_space_project_network, (Accessed 1 May 2019).

Chloe Sterland

[1] S Phadke, 'You Can Be Lonely in a Crowd: The Production of Safety in Mumbai', *Indian Journal of Gender Studies*, vol. 12, no. 1, 2005, pp. 41–62.

Roberto Boettger

Roberto Boettger is an architect based in Rio de Janeiro and London. He studied at the Architectural Association and has worked with 6a architects and OMA. Roberto has been the recipient of the RIBA Wren Scholarship, Valentiny Foundation Award, AA Bursary and commended for the Dennis Sharp Prize and RIBA President's Medal. He has lectured at the AA and other universities. His writings have featured on the *AR, AU, Horizonte, Domus*, and in the book *Supreme Achievement.*

Lewis McNeice

In 2016 Lewis received his bachelor degree in Landscape Architecture at RMIT and, during his final studio, was awarded both the Otto Linne Prize Honorable Mention for Landscape Architecture and the Hamburg Chamber of Architects Award for Interdisciplinary Cooperation. His post-graduate research is focused on issues of resilience and the sustainability of disaster recovery and mitigation. Lewis believes that the built environment is an expression of our shared values and includes growing inequality, unbalanced access to services and developer-lead urban sprawl as slow-onset disasters and unfolding crises. Strongly influenced by land-use and becoming ever more urgent in the face of rapid urbanisation, mass migration and a changing climate, he is interested in the role of landscape architecture as a mitigation tool for cultural competency, engagement and avoiding complacency.

FeiFan Zhang

FeiFan Zhang is an artist and photographer whose work examines how human intentions often result in irreconcilable functions as oddly experienced spaces in the changing urban landscape. She received her MFA in photography from Columbia College Chicago, and BA in English Literature from Beijing International Studies University in Beijing, China, where she was born and raised. Her No Man's Land series has appeared in solo and group exhibitions, as well as digital and printed publications internationally - among which, her work has been featured by Midwest Center for Photography (Wichita, KS) as one of their 2018 emerging photographers, in *Under the Radar* by ArtSlant, and Ground Floor 2018 at Hyde Park Art Center (Chicago, IL).

Sofija Kaljević

Sofija Kaljevic is a Research Assistant in Architecture and Integral Design, at Deakin University, Melbourne, Australia. She has a Doctorate of Philosophy in Human and Community Development from West Virginia University, United States. As well a Master of Architecture from the University of Novi Sad, Serbia. Sofija is also a research associate at MInD Lab, a practice-based and trans-disciplinary research group based in the School of Architecture and Built Environment at Deakin University.

Brent Greene, Abigail Varney

Brent Greene in an associate lecturer in landscape architecture at RMIT and a PhD candidate at the University of Melbourne. Through his work, Brent explores how multiple components of the urban landscape, including nature based phenomena, economic and political systems, impact the conceptualisation and design of urban wildness in public open space. Brent's research has been published in peer reviewed journals such as *Landscape Review* and the *Journal of the International Centre for Landscape and Language*; and he has exhibited in several Melbourne galleries including the National Gallery of Victoria. Brent holds a Masters degree in Landscape Architecture from the University of Melbourne and a Bachelor of Fine Arts (Printmaking) from the Victorian College of the Arts.

Abigail Varney is a documentary photographer based in Melbourne, Australia. Her work predominantly evolves from her connection to mood, colour and scape. After graduating from Photography Studies College in Melbourne 2013, she completed an internship with the late, truly great Mary Ellen Mark in New York City. In 2014, her series of up-and-coming artists featured in the National Portrait Gallery in Canberra. Her long-term documentary project in Coober Pedy 2014 - 2017, was displayed at Sydney's Parliament House, featured at *Head On Photo Festival* Sydney, finalist in the Perimeter small book prize, Moran semi-finalist and announced Landscape Winner at the Centre for Contemporary Photography in Melbourne.

Danielle Toronyi

Danielle Toronyi is a disabled artist, designer, and researcher. She works within the newly emergent research initiative at OLIN, a landscape architecture, urban design, and planning studio based in Philadelphia, Pennsylvania. Her work focuses around making spaces more accessible and resilient for vulnerable people. She understands that designers must confront the structures of power that are responsible for the destruction of the living world and directly impact vulnerable communities. In order to do so, she argues we must work for Black Americans, Latin Americans, Native/Indigenous people, and other POC, as well as the LGBTQIA+, women/femmes, nonbinary folks, immigrants, the disabled, the neurodivergent, the poor, and those of us whose lives exist at the intersection of these experiences. Since 2014 Danielle has volunteered at the Community Design Collaborative, providing pro bono design services for non-profit community organisations in the Philadelphia region. She earned her Master's in Landscape Architecture from North Carolina State University's College of Design in 2012.

Ed Kermode, Dan Parker

Dan Parker is a designer, researcher, and educator at the University of Melbourne. Dan holds a Bachelor of Environments and a Master of Architecture from the University of Melbourne. He teaches and lectures design subjects at the Melbourne School of Design (MSD), and has previously taught at the Monash Art Design & Architecture school (MADA). Specialising in digital design, he works at the Digital Fabrication Laboratory (FabLab) and participates in a cross-disciplinary research group, Deep Design Lab. Dan's research has focused on generative and parametric design, mixed reality, 3D scanning, nonhuman perspectives, interdisciplinary and interspecies collaboration, and geographical information systems. His work has been funded by multiple grants, shown at several conferences and exhibitions, and distinguished through awards in competitions.

Edward Kermode is an architecture graduate from the University of Melbourne currently pursuing his Master of Landscape Architecture at RMIT. Edward is also currently Lead Technical Tutor for an undergraduate subject at the University of Melbourne. He has more than three years experience working at architectural offices both in the United Kingdom and Australia, notably for Grimshaw Architects in London. His time working on large-scale infrastructure and urban design projects in Europe and the Middle East has been a catalyst in his interest towards the socio-political mechanisms shaping todays urban landscapes.

Paige Anderson

Paige Anderson lives in Pittsburgh, Pennsylvania, United States and designs pedestrian and bicycling infrastructure for the City of Pittsburgh's Department of Mobility and Infrastructure. She's also worked at architecture firms and affordable housing non- profits in Seattle, Washington. Hong Kong & the Counter-Production of Spaces Between is derived from her thesis for a Bachelor of Philosophy in Architectural Studies at the University of Pittsburgh. Her professional dedication to urbanism is balanced with a love of nature, spending her weekends on bike tours and traveling to national parks.

Lois Nguyen

Lois Nguyen is a native of Richmond, Virginia and a graduate of Cornell University and a 2019 LAF Olmsted Scholar. Her research is concerned with incorporating disability into community-oriented landscape resiliency. She is currently a landscape designer at Mahan Rykiel Associates in Baltimore, Maryland.

Meremiya Hussein

Meremiya Hussein is an Architectural Design Associate at KDI Kenya. She is passionate about participatory design that socio-economically uplifts communities living in informal settlements. Meremiya is part of the KDI design team that works in partnership with Kibera communities to develop design solutions for productive public spaces. Prior to joining KDI, she successfully led the research, review and development of the sanitation sector brief for the Mukuru Special Planning

Area process, an integrated planning process rooted in collaborative and consultative design. During this project she worked under Sanergy, a social sanitation enterprise based in the Mukuru informal settlement, and in collaboration with fifteen other affiliates, including Nairobi County. Meremiya holds a BA in Architecture from Anadolu University, a certification in Sustainable Water Supply and Sanitation from the University of Jyvaskyla, and a Master's degree in Sustainable Urban Development from Jomo Kenyatta University of Agriculture and Technology.

Charlie Clemoes

Charlie Clemoes is a writer, editor and podcaster from the South West of England, currently living in Amsterdam. He is an editor at Failed Architecture and co- host of the *Failed Architecture* podcast. He is also part of the Amsterdam-based design platform fanfare, principally as co-host of *fanfare tetatet*.

Claire Martin

Claire Martin is a landscape architect and Associate Director of OCULUS' Melbourne studio where she has led the successful delivery of a range of education, health, cultural, infrastructure and public landscape projects. She is a Director of the Australian Institute of Landscape Architects' Board, a member of the Office of the Victorian Government Architect's Victorian Design Review Panel and a contributing editor of Landscape Architecture Australia. Claire is a regular guest lecturer at the Schools of Architecture & Design at the University of Melbourne, and RMIT University where she has taught, is an invited critic, and a member of the Landscape Architecture Program Advisory Committee. She was a Co-Creative Director of This Public Life, the Australian Institute of Landscape Architecture's Festival of Landscape Architecture, which brought together thinkers and practitioners from the arts and sciences.

Emily Schlickman

Emily Schlickman is a landscape and urban designer currently based in the San Francisco Bay Area where she co-leads the research and innovation lab at SWA. Her work on urbanism and infrastructure and has been featured in a range of publications and lectures. She holds a BA in International Studies and Environmental Studies from Washington University in St. Louis and an MLA from the Graduate School of Design at Harvard University where she received the Peter Walker and Partners Fellowship for Landscape Architecture. Formerly, she was an adjunct faculty member at the University of California, Davis.

Sarah Dooling

Dr Sarah Dooling is consultant to policy makers, developers and design professionals. She is an interdisciplinary urban ecologist, who focuses on the equity dimensions of ecological design projects, environmental planning regulations and climate resilience planning. As an independent researcher, her work focuses on strategies to mitigate and ease urban ecological gentrification pressures, the social dynamics of novel urban ecological communities, and equity-focused approaches to climate resilience planning and design.

Chloe Sterland

Chloe Sterland is an RMIT Industrial Design student, currently undertaking her honours project on women and increasing perceptions of safety in public places. Her project is focused on Jewell Station, where she will develop a design intervention to encourage feelings of comfort, exploring how the notion that 'women shouldn't change their behaviour' could be reflected in the design of our public places. She is very interested in how industrial design can be used to tackle social issues such as this. She also enjoys anything to do with making - be it woodwork, leatherwork or ceramics.

Walter Hood

Walther Hood is the creative director and founder of Hood Design Studio, in Oakland, California. He is also a professor of landscape architecture at the University of California, Berkeley. His work is at the intersection of architecture, landscape architecture and fine art, and uses beauty to elucidate idiocracies and strangeness of urban space. Hood Design Studio is a tripartite practice which works across art and fabrication, design and landscape, and research and urbanism. The Studio's award winning work has been featured in publications including *Dwell, The Wall Street Journal,* and *The New York Times.* Walter Hood is also a recipient of the 2017 Academy of Arts and Letters Architecture Award.

Bede Brennan, Minna Leunig

Bede Brennan is a landscape architect and a gardener. He is interested in helping people reconnect with urban nature, and believes design can reinforce and rebuild people's connection to the land. Bede has been lucky to work on a wide range of projects, from renewing historic walking tracks in Northern NSW, to master planning and placemaking in rural Victoria, to model making in collaboration with The University of Melbourne Fablab. Bede has spent time teaching various subjects at the university. He likes to grow vegetables and tend to his chickens.

Minna Leunig is a Melbourne based artist working primarily in black and white and earthy pigments to create playful, primal and earthy images inspired by the natural world - all the way from the dry sclerophyll forests of the Strathbogie ranges to the tangled mangroves and thick rainforests of Cape York. Her work is characterised by a wandering hand and an intuitive lyrical approach to aesthetics. As well as having exhibited at galleries such as Backwoods, Outré, Juddy Roller, Montsalvat, Neon Parlour and Lamington Drive. Minna has a keen interest in bringing art out of gallery spaces and into the public realm through street art, working by the philosophy that art should be an integral part of everyday life, and accessible to all.

Éloïse Choquette

Architect by day, musician and writer by night, community organiser the rest of the time, Éloïse Choquette studied architecture both at Université de Montréal and McGill University, from which they graduated in 2013. Since then, they have worked in a few different architecture firms of various sizes and practices. They have a special interest for institutional and social projects, having worked for many years on construction in Inuit communities in Canada. As a young, queer, disabled, non-binary architect, they have at heart to work towards universal design and accessibility, and promoting inclusive and safer spaces, both in and out of their professional life. For the past fifteen years, they have been involved in different volunteer spaces, community initiatives and social movements. Since 2016, they have been vice-president and a board-member of Rock Camp for Girls and Gender Nonconforming Youth Montreal, for which they are Program Director. Éloïse Choquette lives in Tio'tia:ke, known as Montreal.

Kate Church

Dr Kate Church lectures across the bachelor and masters degrees at RMIT's landscape architecture department, RMIT University, Melbourne. Founder of Floating Studio, her background is in visual arts and landscape architecture. Her research works with film, narrative and and literature to to examine performative materiality of land. She has been published in *Cartography and Narratives, Exposure/00: Design Research in Landscape Architecture and Urban Interior, Informal Explorations, Interventions and Occupations.*

Simone Bliss

Simone Bliss is the Founder and Director of SBLA Studio. She has worked on award-winning, large-scale urban and community-driven projects. Her experience includes twelve years as a Senior Landscape Architect at Taylor Cullity Lethlean (TCL) and two years as an Associate Landscape Architect at Playstreet Studio, based in Hobart. She is highly experienced in masterplanning, concept design, documentation and project management of large- and small-scale projects, bespoke public art installations, and play structures.
Her project experience includes: Bendigo Kangan Tafe Campus, KeepCup Headquarters, Melbourne, Nightingale 2.0 development, Fairfield, Deakin University Reflection Garden, Lilydale High School Entry Precinct and Zoology Building, Collingwood Arts Precinct, System Garden Boardwalk, University of Melbourne, Mandalay Regional Park, Beveridge, Auckland Waterfront (while at TCL), National Arboretum Canberra Pod Playground (while at TCL), North Bank Redevelopment, Launceston (while at Playstreet)

Magdalena Sliwinska

Magdalena Sliwinska is a graduate architect/ landscape architect from the University of Melbourne. She has taught at Swinburne University, Monash (MADA) and University of Melbourne (MSD) across disciplines of interior architecture, architecture and landscape architecture. She is pursuing creative projects that explore how people sense and encounter space on an emotional, spiritual and phenomenological level. Her first paper published by the *Journal of the Interior Design* examined the role of movement and poetry in uncovering the spirit of place and forming an essential part of the design process.

Yazid Ninsalam, Michaela Prescott

Yazid Ninsalam is a lecturer in the Landscape Architecture Program at RMIT. He holds a Doctor of Philosophy in Architecture and was awarded concurrent degrees in Master of Landscape Architecture and Bachelor of Arts (Architecture) with honours from the National University of Singapore. His research foregrounds how landscape architects may deploy ubiquitous terrestrial and aerial sensing methods to produce precise local observations of human-environment conflicts that result from rapid urban transitions.

Dr Michaela Prescott is a landscape architect with experience in both professional and academic contexts. Based in Singapore from 2012-2017, she worked on an interdisciplinary research project on rivers in Indonesia (in landscape ecology) at the Singapore-ETH Centre, completed a doctorate with ETH Zurich, and worked as a landscape architect at HASSELL Singapore. Over the past decade, she has worked in private and commercial practice in Australia, Singapore and the Netherlands, and in municipal landscape design and urban strategic planning in Melbourne, Australia. Prescott's doctorate, ongoing research, design studios and publications primarily focus on the socio-cultural dimensions of landscapes and living environments, and the evolving relation of landscape, infrastructure and urbanisation. She is a Research Fellow and team member on Monash University's current Wellcome Trust and ADB research project, Health and economic benefits of water-sensitive revitalisation in informal urban settlements.

Wendy Scriven

Wendy Scriven lives and works in Melbourne. She is a visual artist and works curating community arts, music and cultural events for young people. The images you see are from Wendy's childhood home. Her experiences have informed her interest in social structures in particular socioeconomic divide.
Her photographic work has included photo essays from the Fitzroy Housing Estate, Sambell Lodge – a home for disadvantaged elderly people and documenting the Kimberley Land Councils Ranger Program, within Western Australia's largest Indigenous community.

The images presented here show Wendy's desire to create a visual narrative that delivers positive stories from uncomfortable spaces.

Zoe Milah DeJesus

Zoe Milah DeJesus is a Melbourne based Puerto-Rican/American artist. Through mixed media painting and digital drawings she draws from her experiences of womanhood. DeJesus uses art as a tool for change, her paintings reflect a world of equality, her aim is to demystify certain ideas about sexuality and give artistic representation to women and the LBGTQ+ community.

PJ Calhoun

PJ grew up surrounded by strong family influences from both art and architecture. They spent their weekends drawing and making models with their father as he was building a landscape architecture practice. Their mother managed art galleries and championed young and emerging talent. They began Calhoun Design this year as an independent design practice. They are currently experimenting with emerging technologies, and interested in their implications for the future of communication design.

Maya Borjesson

Maya Borjesson is a Melbourne-based designer with John Wardle Architects and Artist. She has worked in Architectural studios and Art Galleries in Sydney, Melbourne and London and has been a part of the White Elephant Arts Collective. She works with large scale installation combined with audio and/or projections and has exhibited at Victoria and Albert Museum London, Hackney Wicked London, Light Night London, 1000£ Pend Melbourne and Rancho Notorious Melbourne.

Jixuan (Solomon) Guo

Solomon is a Melbourne based landscape architecture designer/student. His work aims to combine modern design and traditional art. He aims to preserve his own version of the world through his art practise.

Akira Ode-Smith

Akira Ode-Smith is a graduate landscape architect working out of SiteWorks, Brunswick in the collaboratively run experimental design/ research practice, Site Studio. He has exhibited work in Dynamics of Air, Role and most recently Mapping: An Exhibition.

Jieun Lee

Jieun is a South Korean, illustrator based in Suwon. She currently runs her own design label Leegoc as well as teaching art to children. She has featured on online sites such as Its Nice That, Ball Pit Mag and has exhibited at Galleria Faire Seoul Forest. She holds a Bachelor of Fine Art, majoring in Textiles and Metalcraft at Dankook University, Korea and is currently working on illustrating a book.

Chiara Santoro

Chiara Santoro is an Italian self-made artist, born in 1989 in Turin, Italy. At the beginning of her artistic career she experimented with different forms of expression to be able to find the one in which she could feel the most fulfilled, digital graphics. Since 2013 she has established herself as a digital artist through the development of a new, personal and unconventional creative method that includes images made only of pixels and a lot of imagination. As a creative tool, Chiara Santoro uses only her tablet to be able to feel free to start new projects at any time and in any place. She works by structuring her personal visions of the world on the screen, always experimenting with new styles but maintaining a common thread in every work.

Samuel Leighton-Dore

Samuel Leighton-Dore is a queer multidisciplinary artist and writer based on the Gold Coast. With a keen interest in mental health and masculinity, Leighton-Dore writes for SBS Life and produces work spanning ceramics, LED neon, illustration, animation and painting. His book of illustrations, *How To Be A Big Strong Man*, will be released through Smith Street Books and Simon and Schuster in August 2019.

Alice Coates

Alice Coates is a Melbourne-based trained landscape architect. She enjoys illustrating the world around her, and uses her unique style to warp and compare how things are in the world. She is currently studying a Masters of Environment at the University of Melbourne to broaden her scholarship into issues of equity and development.

Carolina Catrola

Carolina Catrola is a thirty-one-year-old storyteller. By dancing between movies, videos and drawings she has managed to survive through her art. She works as a motion designer and an assistant director. She plays as a movie maker and an illustrator.

Fotis Rovolis

Currently based in Athens, Fotis Rovolis deals with space, image, movement and plastic but primarily with sound. He studied architecture in Thessaly, Greece and recently attended courses at the Royal Conservatory and Royal Academy of Arts in the Hague, The Netherlands. He expresses his works via many alias/personas or fictional bands (STRCZDNSMBL, zirlar mord Ω) ending up in multidisciplinary outputs. Triggered by common everyday experiences, exclusions, memories and imaginary utopias, his works respond to the problematics of a white patriarchic, privileged and border-oriented society.